Training
Behavioral
Healthcare
Professionals

The Jossey-Bass
Managed Behavioral Healthcare Library

Michael A. Freeman, General Editor

NOW AVAILABLE

Marketing for Therapists: A Handbook for Success in Managed Care
Jeri Davis, Editor

*The Computerization of Behavioral Healthcare: How to Enhance
Clinical Practice, Management, and Communications*
Tom Trabin, Editor

*Behavioral Risk Management: How to Avoid Preventable Losses
from Mental Health Problems in the Workplace*
Rudy M. Yandrick

*Training Behavioral Healthcare Professionals:
Higher Learning in the Era of Managed Care*
James M. Schuster, Mark R. Lovell, and Anthony M. Trachta, Editors

*The Ethical Way: Challenges and Solutions for Managed
Behavioral Healthcare*
H. Steven Moffic

The Complete Capitation Handbook
Gayle L. Zieman, Editor

*Inside Outcomes: The National Review of Behavioral
Healthcare Outcomes*
Tom Trabin, Michael A. Freeman, and Michael Pallak

*Managed Behavioral Healthcare:
History, Models, Strategic Challenges, and Future Course*
Michael A. Freeman and Tom Trabin

*Behavioral Group Practice Performance Characteristics:
The Council of Group Practices Benchmarking Study*
Allen Daniels, Teresa Kramer, and Nalini Mahesh

*How to Respond to Managed Behavioral Healthcare:
A Workbook Guide for Your Organization*
Barbara Mauer, Dale Jarvis, Richard Mockler, and Tom Trabin

Training Behavioral Healthcare Professionals

Higher Learning in the Era of Managed Care

James M. Schuster
Mark R. Lovell
Anthony M. Trachta
Editors
Foreword by Michael A. Freeman
General Editor

Jossey-Bass Publishers • San Francisco

Substantial discounts on bulk quantities of Jossey-Bass books are
available to corporations, professional associations, and other
organizations. For details and discount information, contact the
special sales department at Jossey-Bass Inc., Publishers,
(415) 433–1740; Fax (800) 605–2665.

For sales outside the United States, please contact your local
Simon & Schuster International Office.

Jossey-Bass Web address: http://www.josseybass.com

 Manufactured in the United States of America on Lyons Falls
Turin Book. This paper is acid-free and 100 percent totally
chlorine-free.

Library of Congress Cataloging-in-Publication Data

Training behavioral healthcare professionals: higher learning in the era
of managed care / James M. Schuster, Mark R. Lovell, Anthony M.
Trachta, editors; foreword by Michael A. Freeman.
p.   cm.—(The Jossey-Bass managed behavioral healthcare library)
Includes bibliographical references and index.
ISBN 0-7879-0795-2
1. Mental health personnel—Training of—United States.
2. Managed mental health care—United States. 3. Psychotherapists—
Training of—United States. I. Schuster, James M., [date]. II. Lovell,
Mark R., [date]. III. Trachta, Anthony M., [date]. IV. Series.
RC459.5.U6T73   1997
616.89'0071'173—DC20

FIRST EDITION
HB Printing   10 9 8 7 6 5 4 3 2 1

Contents

Foreword

Behavioral healthcare has changed. The old and once familiar professional landscape now seems altered and disorienting. The familiar landmarks that were well known to mental health administrators, clinicians, insurance executives, employee assistance program directors, and academic researchers are fading off the map. Vanishing or gone are the employers who did not pay attention to healthcare costs, the insurance plans that would reimburse on a fee-for-service basis, the hospitals with beds filled with patients whose coverage encouraged lengthy stays, the solo clinicians with full practices of affluent patients seeking long-term insight-oriented therapy, and the community mental health centers that worked in a system of their own.

The scenery of today is different. Health maintenance organizations and managed behavioral health plans have replaced the insurance companies. Employers and purchasing cooperatives are bypassing even these new organizations and purchasing directly from providers. Clinicians are forming group practices. Groups are affiliating with facilities. Facilities are forming integrated delivery systems. Integrated delivery systems are building organized systems of care that include insurance, care management, and service delivery functions. Information systems are linking payers, managers, and providers into coordinated and comprehensive systems with new levels of accountability. The boundaries of the public sector are eroding, and the distinction between public and private has become more difficult to perceive.

Adjusting to this "brave new world" is challenging, and many mental health professionals are being tempted to give up and opt out now. But for most of us, the challenge is worth facing. While this period is fraught with difficulty and risk, there are also a number of opportunities. Whenever a paradigm shifts, those having a stake in the previous paradigm risk losing their place in the one that emerges. The Jossey-Bass Managed Behavioral Healthcare Library will help you identify and confront the challenges you will face as the prevailing healthcare paradigms change. Moreover, the volumes in this library will provide you with pragmatic strategies and solutions that you can call upon to sustain your importance in the healthcare systems of the future.

In spite of the upheavals transforming the behavioral healthcare enterprise in this country, many of its basic goals remain the same. In fact, managed behavioral healthcare has come about largely because our previous way of doing things failed to solve fundamental problems related to the cost, quality, accessibility, and outcomes of care. "Managed behavioral healthcare"—whatever this concept may eventually come to mean—holds out the promise of affordable, appropriate, and effective mental health and addiction treatment services for all. The various initiatives and efforts that are under way to reach this new service plateau will result in a vast array of professional opportunities for the behavioral healthcare specialists whose talents are required to make this promise come true.

By reading the books and reports in the Managed Behavioral Healthcare Library, you will learn how to respond to the perils and possibilities presented by today's shift to managed behavioral healthcare. The authors of this book and of the other volumes in this series recognize the need for direct and pragmatic solutions to the challenges posed by the changing paradigms of behavioral healthcare financing and services. To help you meet this need and obtain the resources and solutions you require, each chapter of each publication is written by an outstanding expert who can communicate in a pragmatic style to help you make a difference and meet each of the key challenges posed by the new landscape in behavioral healthcare.

This volume and the others planned for the series help you

improve your effectiveness at pricing, financing, and delivering high-quality, cost-effective care. Future volumes will also provide straightforward solutions to the ethical challenges of managed behavioral healthcare and offer advice about practice management and marketing during a period of industry consolidation. You can look forward to still other books and reports about developing and managing a group practice, creating workplace-based behavioral healthcare programs, measuring outcomes, computerizing delivery systems, and ways of "benchmarking" in order to compare your organization or practice with others that face similar challenges.

Because the landscape of behavioral healthcare is in flux, professionals in the field need to be aware of alternative scenarios of the future and develop the skill sets for success within each one. For behavioral healthcare leaders, it is critical to have the vision to select the best options that accord with shared values and to have the skills to put these possibilities into practice. For this reason, the themes of vision, action, and results are incorporated into the volumes you read in the Managed Behavioral Healthcare Library.

Vision

In the context of the current debate and upheavals in healthcare, we have seen broad agreement regarding the importance of behavioral health scrutiny at an affordable price for all Americans. The Managed Behavioral Healthcare Library offers publications that show how universal coverage for affordable, appropriate, accessible, and effective mental health and addiction treatment benefits and services can be achieved.

Methods

How can we put into operation the new paradigms, the new models and systems of care needed to make the promise of managed care come true? New methods of benefit administration and health services delivery will be required to implement this vision within realistic financial limits.

At the broadest level, these methods include the core technologies used to manage benefits, care, and the health status of individuals and defined populations. At the level of frontline operations, these methods include continuous quality improvement, process reengineering, outcomes management, public-private integration, computerization, and delivery system reconfiguration in the context of capitation financing. These are the areas in which the Managed Behavioral Healthcare Library helps you build skill sets.

New methods of direct clinical care are also required. Instead of treating episodes of illness, clinicians in future managed and integrated behavioral healthcare systems will use disease-state management methods to reduce morbidity and mortality for individuals and for groups. The Managed Behavioral Healthcare Library provides frontline clinicians and delivery system managers with the skills that will enable our healthcare systems to truly provide scientifically validated bio-psycho-social treatment of choice in behavioral healthcare.

Action and Results

Knowing that we are in a period of change, and even having the desire to make the changes that are needed, makes little difference without actions based on methods that can produce results. Because you take action and produce results through day-in, day-out application of your professional expertise, the Managed Behavioral Healthcare Library is action oriented, to provide the greatest possible benefit to you and your colleagues.

—⁓—

In light of the dramatic changes in the behavioral healthcare field, the most appropriate methods used to educate behavioral healthcare professionals must be reevaluated and restructured. It simply does not make sense to concentrate training in in-patient settings when on-line, ambulatory, and home-based care is favored within managed care arrangements. Extensive education in long-term treatment skills should give way to opportunities for learning brief and problem-focused therapy, psychoeducational and group interventions, and self-help referral skills.

Similarly, the core content of graduate and post-graduate clinical education must be reconfigured in order to prepare today's clinicians in training for the behavioral healthcare workplace of tomorrow. Clinicians in training today will need to have the skills and capabilities required to measure and manage outcomes, follow and improve clinical practice guidelines, capture data in electronic medical records, and participate in interdisciplinary treatment teams.

Fortunately, the editors and authors of *Training Behavioral Healthcare Professionals: Higher Learning in the Era of Managed Care* identify these challenges and propose solutions. This highly accomplished group of frontline and forward-looking educators brings us directly in contact with the most managed care oriented training models that are currently in place, while outlining the alternatives and preferred pathways for academic programs and continuing clinical education services.

In this book you will learn about the impact of managed care on graduate and post-graduate training in psychiatry, psychiatric nursing, psychology, and social work. James Schuster, Mark Lovell, Anthony Trachta, and their colleagues outline the new curriculum requirements of advanced clinical education, and the methods by which these curricula can be implemented. They also illustrate the perspective of the managed care company, reviewing the ways in which managed care organizations view academic behavioral healthcare training and research.

We have designed this book, along with the other volumes in the Managed Behavioral Healthcare Library, to provide the information and inspiration essential for all professionals who want to understand the challenges and opportunities available today.

Tiburon, California Michael A. Freeman
November 1996

*We would like to dedicate
this book to our wives:
Cathy, Eileen, and Joyce*

Introduction

The development of managed healthcare systems is causing dramatic changes in the education and practices of mental health professionals. Though at times these shifts have been very frustrating to me, as they are to many clinicians, at other times I have found them fascinating and welcome.

My introduction to unmanaged care occurred on the first day of my psychiatry residency in 1986. During the morning report that day I discovered that a patient who was ready for discharge would not be discharged until later in the week because there was not yet another patient ready to be admitted to that bed!

During the next several months I was surprised at the variety of healthcare systems designed at least partly for the convenience or financial benefit of providers rather than patients. Patients were hospitalized for weeks before starting active medical treatment because of the requirements of treatment protocols. Outpatient appointments could require waits of several weeks. On weekends many inpatients never saw attending physicians or had adjustments in their treatment. I worked in a very competitive real estate business before medical school, and I was surprised that enterprises that were not very "customer friendly" could thrive. Medical care appeared immune from the rules of classic economics.

During my residency I began to read about the growing impact of managed care on the West Coast. It had not yet had a major effect on the Pittsburgh area where I was training, but it was widely recognized as a very different paradigm for care that would eventually enter our region. I hoped (and still do hope) that some way could be found to incorporate the positive effects of managed care, such as the requirement to provide more cost-effective and patient-friendly services, while maintaining high-quality care.

To better understand these issues, I pursued an M.B.A. degree during my residency program. I learned that businesspeople approach problems in a very pragmatic, solution-oriented way. This problem-solving process differs significantly from the medical approach, in which great time and resources are spent in order to find the "best" answer; for example, businesspeople faced with a service delivery issue typically gather readily available information and make a prompt decision. Physicians seem much more likely to spend much time performing studies to gather additional information before deciding on their course of action.

After completing my residency program I began to work as a consultation psychiatrist at another tertiary care hospital in Pittsburgh, Allegheny General Hospital (AGH), where I am still on staff today. Shortly before my arrival, AGH became affiliated with the Medical College of Pennsylvania in Philadelphia and several other hospitals in the Philadelphia area as part of the Allegheny Health, Education, and Research Foundation system. Medical students regularly trained in our service. Four years ago our department initiated a psychiatry residency program and now, in addition to providing training in consultation and emergency psychiatry for these residents, I am responsible for their training in administrative psychiatry.

My work with psychiatry residents has highlighted several concerns for me. First, most residents receive little or no formal training in administrative and economic issues in medical school. This omission leaves them unprepared for the issues of efficiency and cost-effectiveness that they must begin to grapple with as residents. Second, many aspects of managed care systems, such as service preauthorization and benefit limitations, cause as much frustration for residents as they do for other providers and can disillusion them about their career choice. Finally, despite their frustrations, residents are usually eager to learn about managed care systems and about how they can provide the best possible care for patients within those systems.

My coeditors, Mark Lovell and Anthony (Tony) Trachta, and I have attempted to outline the opportunities and challenges that currently face behavioral health educators as they prepare trainees to practice in managed healthcare systems. These areas include both clinical and financial issues. Though the required changes in education will, at times, be difficult, failure to complete them will lead to inadequate training for our students.

Overview of the Contents

This book describes the forces shaping the training of behavioral healthcare professionals today. In Chapter One, I outline the effect of managed care on behavioral healthcare and on the education of behavioral healthcare trainees including psychiatrists, psychologists, social workers, and nurses. In Chapter Two, Ole Thienhaus details the impact of managed care on the training of psychiatry residents and describes new perspectives on residency training. Chapter Three, a complementary chapter by Marcia Kaplan, reviews several practical, pragmatic, and creative approaches to addressing these issues.

Challenges in the training of psychologists are discussed in Chapter Four by David Shaw, who currently directs a psychology internship program. In Chapter Five, Mark Lovell outlines further approaches to be used in clinical training in psychology.

Many behavioral health professionals at the master's degree level, including social workers and nurses, have a variety of educational and training options. In Chapter Six, Anthony Trachta reviews the historical roots of social work, the limitations of this education and training in a managed care environment, and options that can strengthen the field of social work while it adapts to a new environment. In Chapter Seven, Carole Taylor reviews the role of nursing in behavioral health and modifications in nursing training that will be required to secure its continued viability.

The book concludes with two administrative perspectives. Mark Fuller, a medical director of a managed care company, explains concerns held by managed care companies about the education of current healthcare professionals. He further explores how these educational limitations have translated into difficulties for practitioners treating patients who have managed insurance. The final chapter is written by Deborah Teplow, director of the Institute for Behavioral Healthcare. She outlines current limitations in the continuing education of mental health professionals and several opportunities, especially regarding effective practice patterns in managed care systems.

We believe this book identifies and highlights many of the current problems facing behavioral health educators and shares some of the creative ideas educators have developed to resolve them. We hope it serves as a useful resource for those working to develop, change, and improve education programs for mental health practitioners.

Acknowledgments

We would like to acknowledge Michael Freeman for his help in the development of the concept for this book. In addition, we want to thank our editors, Alan Rinzler and Katie Levine, for their great expertise and assistance.

Pittsburgh, Pennsylvania   JAMES M. SCHUSTER
November 1996

Training
Behavioral
Healthcare
Professionals

Chapter One

The Development of Managed Care

James M. Schuster

Since the mid-1980s there have been dramatic changes in the healthcare system of the United States. These changes have been driven by new funding mechanisms of healthcare insurance and healthcare services.[1] Most Americans were once covered by indemnity insurance, which allowed them to visit physicians and hospitals of their choice and permitted physicians to prescribe any indicated procedure or hospitalization. Providers were paid "usual and customary" charges and institutions were paid at least enough to cover their costs.

This system of generous funding and reimbursement enabled millions of Americans to work in relatively well-paid health service positions and assisted in funding their education. For example, although tuition for some medical schools and graduate programs in psychology is more than $10,000 per year, this tuition rarely pays for more than a small portion of the total educational costs of these professionals. The remaining costs were paid by Medicare and other public funding, supplemented by other revenues from clinical services. This system of generous reimbursement is now ending.

Patients' insurance now is often provided by health maintenance organizations (HMOs) or preferred provider organizations (PPOs). More than 65 million Americans currently have these forms of insurance and most Americans will probably be covered by them within the next few years. These insurance plans usually provide much lower reimbursement for specific services than indemnity insurance paid. This decrease in reimbursement has significantly lowered the amount of money that institutions can devote to offsetting educational expenses.

Reimbursement of academic psychiatrists by non-managed insurers is also stagnant or declining. Medicare, for example, has recently issued new guidelines that effectively limit the amount of resident psychiatrist activity that an attending psychiatrist can supervise and bill for.

HMOs and PPOs also limit the number of services that can be provided to patients by imposing benefit limitations, financial incentives, or utilization review.[2] These restrictions have led to significant changes in practice patterns. Patients are hospitalized less often, receive more care on an outpatient basis, and receive treatments that are designed to improve their symptoms and function quickly.

Some healthcare providers have sought to ameliorate these limitations on reimbursement and practice patterns by contracting directly with employers. These providers are usually part of multidisciplinary groups that include psychiatrists, psychologists, and health professionals at the master's degree level such as social workers and nurses. They often work closely with hospitals or other medical groups in these contracts in which the providers become, in essence, the insurer as well as the provider.

These contracts typically involve capitation with both its benefits and risks. In capitated contracts, a provider entity receives a fixed sum per month from an employer or insurer for providing any services required by a specified population. The sum remains the same each month, regardless of how many services are utilized by the population. In theory, these contracts allow the group to capture profit that is otherwise absorbed by the insurer. These arrangements require both clinical and administrative sophistication. In addition, insurers may see such provider groups as competitors. If insurers eliminate these groups from their networks, the referral base of the group is threatened.

These alterations in practice patterns and funding have created many problems with the traditional ways of funding education for health professionals, curricula in traditional training programs, and employment of program graduates.[3] They also have led training programs to rethink their goals and expectations for their graduates and this process is creating new opportunities for trainees.

PPOs, HMOs, and Changes in Reimbursement

The driving force behind the changes in healthcare is the desire to limit costs. Healthcare now consumes more than 14 percent of the gross national product and a much higher proportion of employee health benefit plans.[4] To limit expenditures, private corporations and government organizations both at the state and federal level are offering or requiring employees and citizens to enroll in managed care entities.

Some questions remain about the effectiveness of HMOs and PPOs at limiting expenses after an initial savings at the time of enrollment. In addition, serious concerns have been raised about how the organization and delivery of care affects the quality of that care, especially among indigent and chronically ill populations.[5] However, payers (employers, government organizations, and insurers) believe that managed care systems offer the best chance to limit healthcare expenditures.

Preferred Provider Organizations

The PPO was the first widespread form of managed care, and many patients were enrolled in them by the mid-1980s. PPOs typically limit the number of providers and hospitals from whom a patient can seek care. However, PPOs usually do not limit the utilization of healthcare services by those physicians or provide financial incentives for those providers to decrease expensive procedures. Providers continue to be paid on a fee-for-service basis, though the rates are typically reduced from typical indemnity rates. Although they were used widely during the 1980s, PPOs failed to significantly slow the growth of healthcare costs and the alternative model of HMOs has grown in popularity.

Health Maintenance Organizations

HMOs, which were founded in the early twentieth century, are like PPOs in that they restrict the choice of providers and hospitals. HMO networks of professional and institutional providers usually are more limited than those of PPOs. In addition, HMOs strive to reduce the utilization of services including visits to providers, laboratory and radiologic evaluations, and especially hospitalizations.

Activities designed to reduce services fall under the rubric of utilization management.[6] Utilization management typically includes both direct oversight by insurance company reviewers of services (utilization review) and payment mechanisms designed to reduce utilization. Although both activities are focused on reduction in utilization, they are thought to increase the quality and cost-effectiveness of care.

Utilization Review

Utilization review includes review of expensive services (including hospitalization) by nurses and physicians. For example, when patients require hospitalization, the provider (medical professional or hospital) is often required to call the insurance company to obtain authorization for payment. Though the provider can treat the patient without authorization, many insurance companies will refuse to pay for the services unless the preauthorization process has been completed.

After the provider calls, the insurance company nurses and physicians determine whether or not the hospitalization meets the company's "medical necessity criteria." These criteria have largely redefined the rationale for hospitalization. Patients once were hospitalized if it appeared that the hospital was the site where they could receive "the best" care. However, the underlying principle of utilization review criteria is that the service must be "medically necessary" for patients to receive adequate care; if it is possible for the patient to safely receive care in an outpatient setting, then inpatient care is considered inappropriate.[7,8]

A forty-three-year-old woman presents to the emergency department with a five-month history of progressively increasing depressive symptoms including poor energy, difficulty going to work, sleep
disturbance, frequent crying spells, and thoughts of dying. She does
not have any suicidal plan or intent. She has not had any treatment
and agrees to be admitted to the hospital. When called for preauthorization, the insurance reviewer refuses to provide coverage for
hospital care. The patient denies she poses any risk to herself, so the
reviewer authorizes only outpatient care even though it may lead to
slower improvement of the patient's symptoms and function.

As this case illustrates, when a provided service fails to meet its
criteria, an insurance company often will deny payment for services. The provider can still render the service, but the insurer will
not pay for it and the patient is responsible for the cost.

Utilization review has some effectiveness in reducing costs, but
is limited by the fact that the reviewer's information is usually
derived from chart assessment or phone conversations. Reviewers
may deny care inappropriately because of inadequate information,
whereas providers may try to "slant" the information they provide
to reviewers in order to receive approval. In addition, utilization
review often creates an adversarial interaction between the insurer
and the provider. Healthcare providers and insurers may use different definitions of "medical necessity" that make it difficult for them
to work collaboratively.

Financial Incentives

Many HMOs have moved from away from individual case review
because of its limited effectiveness and administrative expense.
Instead, they are offering financial incentives for providers to limit
costs. Financial incentives appear to be both more efficient
(because they require less administrative infrastructure) and more
effective than utilization review. These arrangements allow the
provider to share the financial risk of the insurer.

The primary form of risk sharing is capitation. Capitation has several advantages for providers. First, payments in fee-for-service systems have undergone significant reductions and often barely cover providers' costs. Capitation can allow providers to capture more total revenue if they can deliver services efficiently. Second, capitation typically frees providers from intrusive utilization review efforts by insurance companies. Third, capitation allows providers to protect or gain market share.

There are also potential problems with capitation. It creates significant financial risks for the provider and can lead to considerable financial losses if the negotiated capitated rate is too low or if, through random selection, the capitated population requires an unusually high number of services in the defined time period. There are ways to minimize this risk through contract negotiation, but it cannot be eliminated entirely and groups that engage in capitation must have substantial financial reserves.

An additional potential problem is that capitation may lead to inadequate treatment. Under a fee-for-service system, providers have a financial incentive to provide more services and increase their revenues. However, every service provided under a capitation agreement increases the provider's costs and there is a strong incentive to provide brief, focused treatments. The following case describes how this arrangement can create incentives to "undertreat" patients.

A seventeen-year-old girl is admitted to a pediatric unit after taking an overdose of a benzodiazepine. The overdose occurred after an argument with her parents about her boyfriend. The patient acknowledges that she intended to die at the time of the overdose, though she denies being suicidal when she is seen the next day. Her history of depressive symptoms is unclear. The consulting psychiatrist wishes to transfer her to an inpatient psychiatric unit for forty-eight hours of observation, and the patient and her family agree with that plan. The psychiatric unit, which is run by a capitated provider, refuses to admit the patient because the patient is no longer suicidal. The capitated system will treat the patient only in an outpatient setting.

Though such stringent limitations on services and the consequent questions about quality could haunt a capitated provider in the long term, financial results are typically judged on a short-term basis.

To avoid inappropriate restrictions on treatment, quality assessment has been added to cost-effectiveness as a measure of the outcome of managed care in general and capitation agreements in particular. However, reliable measurement of outcomes in heterogenous, non-controlled populations is difficult and outcomes assessment does not yet drive care management. The demonstration of good outcome is likely to assume greater significance as the costs of care continue to fall and become relatively uniform among providers.

Managed Care and Behavioral Healthcare

Managed care has, to date, probably had a more dramatic impact on the delivery of behavioral healthcare services than on other areas of medicine. First, behavioral healthcare probably has been more vulnerable to limitations because it has traditionally had "second-class" status within the healthcare system. There has been a stigma associated with behavioral healthcare services within the healthcare system as there is within society at large. In addition, most indemnity insurance plans have much more limited benefits for mental health services than for other medical care. For example, mental health benefits in indemnity plans typically have been limited to thirty inpatient days per year and $20 to $50 per outpatient visit, whereas benefits for other medical care have been much more generous. In addition, the costs of some areas of behavioral health, especially inpatient care of adolescents and inpatient drug rehabilitation, exploded during the 1980s and payers were eager to decrease their utilization.

The rise in costs, combined with relatively limited benefits, has led to very stringent utilization review for inpatient psychiatric services by managed care organizations (MCOs). MCOs have often expanded outpatient benefits beyond those found in indemnity plans.[9] However, they typically use relatively limited networks of providers and subject outpatient services to a utilization review process that can be cumbersome for both providers and patients.[10]

These benefit and utilization limitations have caused several changes in the delivery of behavioral healthcare. First, there is now a great emphasis on limiting inpatient services and treating patients in outpatient settings whenever possible.[11] The number of inpatient days per year for behavioral health services per thousand enrolled members often falls from 130 days in indemnity plans to 20 days in HMOs.[12]

This emphasis on alternatives to inpatient care has fostered the development of a wide range of other levels of treatment. There has been significant growth of partial and day hospital programs, intensive outpatient programs, emergency services, and in-home and crisis services. The focus of these services is to treat patients in the least intensive level of care possible. The rationale for care has shifted from providing the "best possible" care to "medically necessary" care.

To further limit costs, MCOs have moved as much care as possible to the least expensive providers. The practical effect of this strategy, in behavioral healthcare, has been to shift most psychotherapeutic services from psychiatrists and doctorate-level psychologists to providers at the master's degree level, especially social workers and nurses.[13] Psychiatrists are used sparingly in the delivery of care in managed mental health systems. Their roles primarily include diagnostic formulation, psychopharmacology, and supervision of other providers.[14] The following case describes how psychiatrists are often discouraged from providing psychotherapy.

Mr. J. was a forty-one-year-old man with borderline traits and a chronic depressive disorder. He had seen his psychiatrist for ten years for medication maintenance. In addition, he had fifteen psychotherapy sessions per year with the psychiatrist, usually when he had a personal crisis. When the patient called his new insurance carrier, he was told that he could continue to see the psychiatrist for medication assessments, because the psychiatrist was in the insurer's network, but that he would need to see a master's-level provider for psychotherapy, because that company did not approve psychiatric visits for psychotherapy.

As the drive to lower costs continues, doctorate-level psychologists are finding increasing questions from insurers about their role as psychotherapists. Master's-level providers typically cost 20 to 30 percent less than these psychologists, so many insurance companies primarily utilize master's-level providers for therapy and utilize doctorate-level psychologists primarily for psychological testing. Other companies pay only one rate for psychotherapy sessions, regardless of the educational background of the provider.

Providers are reacting to these changes in several ways. First, they are moving from small, often solo practices, to group settings. The percentage of psychiatrists who practice in group settings has increased significantly in recent years. In addition, mental health providers are often forming multidisciplinary practices that include psychiatrists, psychologists, and master's-level professionals. These multi-specialty groups allow delivery of the full range of outpatient professional services desired by MCOs and will likely be the most cost-effective form of care delivery.

Second, providers are offering more focused treatments such as cognitive-behavioral therapy and interpersonal therapy, and fewer are offering open-ended psychodynamic treatments. Though many providers continue to adhere to psychodynamic principles, they are less likely to discourage patient-initiated termination and less likely to interpret it as resistance to treatment.

The Effect of Managed Care on Professional Identity

The development of managed care has led to significant changes in how providers view themselves and their treatment of patients. In the past, providers generally believed—especially if they used a psychodynamic model—that more treatment was usually better and that it was their professional obligation to both recommend and provide extended treatment for many, if not most, patients. This underlying assumption has been dramatically challenged by MCOs, which ask providers to focus on improvement of the patient's functioning in relatively brief periods of time. Managed care's thrust toward short-term treatment is supported by studies that have examined brief, focused treatments for acute depressive and anxiety disorders. However, few studies have examined the effectiveness of short-term treatment modalities for patients with chronic psychiatric illnesses. These are the patients who utilize most of the financial resources spent on behavioral healthcare.

The roles of clinicians have also changed significantly in reaction to the changes in these practice patterns. Psychiatrists have a very limited role in the psychotherapeutic treatment of patients whose care is funded by managed care insurance plans.[15] In the past, psychiatrists provided only psychotherapy to many patients and combined pharmaceutical therapy with psychotherapy when indicated. However, many MCOs do not refer patients to psychiatrists if patients do not require pharmacotherapy and they expect most patient contact by psychiatrists to be "medication visits."

Psychologists continue to receive referrals for psychotherapy from most MCOs. However, the increment between payment for therapy from psychologists and from master's-level providers is slowly disappearing. Many companies may eventually offer one rate for psychotherapy, regardless of the qualifications of the professional. In addition, many MCOs try to limit psychological testing, and much testing of children for attentional and behavioral problems is not covered by managed insurance plans.

Master's-level providers have assumed more responsibility for psychotherapeutic treatments and are providing psychotherapy for severely ill patients who would have seen psychologists or psychiatrists in the past. Master's-level providers and physicians often work together in treatment teams to combine psychotherapeutic and psychopharmacologic treatments when clinically indicated.

Managed care also has dramatically changed the way that clinicians think about outcomes and quality. This issue used to be determined only on a case-by-case basis. However, utilizing the concepts of Continuous Quality Improvement (CQI), managed care has pushed clinicians to focus on measuring the outcomes of populations. These outcomes include the rehospitalization rate and use of inpatient and outpatient resources. Many practices have started formal outcomes programs that drive their utilization management programs.

Case Management

Multidisciplinary treatment teams usually use case management to provide effective collaboration and coordination of care.[16] In the past, care given by different providers was often uncoordinated and sporadic. To decrease costs, much care, especially of patients with severe and persistent illnesses, is now provided in systems with a strong case management component.

Case managers, who are typically practitioners with bachelor's or master's degrees, have several functions. First, they seek to ensure that care from various providers is well coordinated and that they complement each other. Second, they often try to increase patient compliance so that patients are less likely to relapse and require intensive treatments. In some instances, with chronically mentally ill patients, case managers even try to address psychosocial issues such as housing and education which may exacerbate patients' illnesses. Participation in such efforts provides an outstanding opportunity for trainees to better understand that treatment efforts can be cost-effective.

New Goals for Educational Programs

Changes in the financing and delivery of behavioral healthcare services due to the development of managed care have created many new demands in the education of mental health professionals. First, educational programs must address and explain the issues of financing and cost-effectiveness explicitly. Many programs once ignored these issues or even denigrated them as activities that should be left to "administrators." Thorough understanding of these issues means that trainees must be taught the basics of economics and practice management. In addition, they must understand the relative costs and the relative effectiveness of various forms of treatment and how to develop the most cost-effective treatment plan for individual patients. Successful application and understanding of these concepts require the best clinical skills as well as the ability to apply economic principles.

Notes

1. Trabin, T., & Freeman, M. (1995). Core methods and predominant models. In T. Trabin & M. Freeman (Eds.), *Managed behavioral healthcare* (pp. 1–6). Tiburon, CA: Centralink Publishers.
2. Rodwin, M. (1995). Conflicts in managed care. *New England Journal of Medicine, 332*, 604–606.
3. Anders, G. (1995, March 17). Once a hot specialty, anesthesiology cools as insurers scale back. *Wall Street Journal*, pp. A1, A4.
4. Schuster, J. M. (1993). Managed care and mental health services: Lessons for health care providers. *Journal of Medical Quality, 8*, 200–203.
5. McFarland, B. H. (1994). Health maintenance organizations and persons with severe mental illness. *Community Mental Health Journal, 30*, 221–242.
6. Tischler, G. L. (1990). Utilization management of mental health services by private third parties. *American Journal of Psychiatry, 147*, 967–973.

7. Borenstein, D. B. (1995). Managed care: A means of rationing psychiatric treatment. *Hospital and Community Psychiatry, 41*, 1095–1098; Sederer, L., & Summergrad, P. (1993). Criteria for hospital admission. *Hospital and Community Psychiatry, 44*, 116–118.

8. Geraty, R., Bartlett, J., Hill, E., Lee, F., Shusterman, A., & Waxman, A. (1994, March/April). The impact of managed behavioral healthcare on the costs of psychiatric and chemical dependency treatment. *Behavioral Healthcare Tomorrow,* 18–30.

9. Goldstein, L. S. (1989). Genuine managed care in psychiatry: A proposed practice model. *General Hospital Psychiatry, 11*, 271–277.

10. Cooper, H. (1993, September 1). Cost controls impel psychiatric hospitals to establish more outpatient programs. *Wall Street Journal,* pp. B1, B8.

11. Melek, S., & Pyenson, B. (1995). Actuarially determined capitation rates for mental health benefits. Washington, DC: American Psychiatric Association.

12. Schuster, J. M., Kern, E. E., Kane, V., & Nettleman, L. (1994). Changing roles of mental health clinicians in multidisciplinary teams. *Hospital and Community Psychiatry, 45*, 1187–1189.

13. Sharfstein, S. (1994). Economics redefining the practice of psychiatry. *Bulletin of the Menninger Clinic, 58*, 447–452.

14. Lazarus, A. (1994). Ten reasons why psychiatrists may dislike managed competition. *Hospital and Community Psychiatry, 45*, 496–498.

15. Panzarino, P. J., & Wetherbee, D. G. (1990, November). Advanced case management in mental health: Quality and efficiency combined. *Quality Review Bulletin, 16*, 386–390.

Chapter Two

Managed Care's Impact on Psychiatric Residency Training

Ole J. Thienhaus

As a clinical educator in medical schools, I have been forced to keep abreast of developments in the environment where such education occurs. In the beginning of 1996, I moved from the vice-chair's position of the department of psychiatry at the University of Cincinnati, where managed care is ubiquitous, to Reno, Nevada, where managed care has only begun to penetrate the healthcare market. In the brief time that I have served as chairman of the department of psychiatry at the University of Nevada School of Medicine, I have come to believe that northern Nevada will catch up with other parts of the country in terms of managed care.

In order to be prepared and put my previous experiences in context, I undertook extensive literature searches. I found that the impact of managed care on access to healthcare, on treatment choices, on patient satisfaction, and on cost has received ample attention in the literature. I counted almost 1,900 indexed articles on the topic of managed care for 1987 through 1993, and the trend is rising.[1] Managed care's effects on research and education have been addressed less thoroughly.

Academic medicine is ultimately judged by the quality of its "products"—the generation of new knowledge and the expertise of its trainees. Research and education relate to future quality and directions of the healthcare sector. Therefore, outcome measures become available only in the long run, years after changes in the delivery system have occurred. For the time being, relevant observations must primarily focus on system-related influences on the processes of medical education and investigation, occasionally complemented by speculative reflections about possible results in the future.

Changes in the healthcare delivery system affect clinical training sites, curricular content, access to patient care, and funding. In this chapter I will address the issues involved in training medical graduates who are residents and fellows. I will try to highlight changes against the background of current regulatory requirements. In conclusion, I will address the more general question of professional identity and how it is defined by our approach to graduate professional training.

Current Requirements in Psychiatric Training

The current training criteria include a minimum of four months' full-time equivalent (FTE) in primary care and at least two months in neurology (generally in the first postgraduate year) and no more than six to eight months of first-year psychiatry.[2] All first-year rotations can be hospital- or outpatient-based. The second through fourth years specify nine to eighteen months FTE in inpatient psychiatry, twelve months or more of outpatient psychiatry (to include both short-term and long-term experiences), and at least two months each of both consultation and child or adolescent psychiatry, respectively.

The differentiation of inpatient and outpatient psychiatry as distinct areas of training in the latter part of the syllabus is noteworthy. Long-term psychotherapy is operationalized as at least one year of weekly or more frequent "sessions" and thus presumably means insight-oriented therapy. The fact that this specific requirement has been retained as a fundamental aspect of training is a reminder of the historical origins of residency training in psychiatry during the heyday of psychoanalysis in the decades immediately following World War II.

Changes that have already occurred include the greater emphasis on emergency psychiatry and consultation training and the inclusion of experiences and formal didactics addressing the fiscal aspects of behavioral healthcare as specified in Section B.1. of the Residency Review Committee Guidelines.[3]

Changes in the Healthcare Delivery System

Changes in Clinical Training Sites

In the psychiatric emergency service in Cincinnati, we had a third-year resident managing patients on site. One day, the resident wanted to refer a patient with alcohol dependency to a twenty-eight-day inpatient alcohol treatment program. The treatment program was ready to accept the patient, but requested that the resident first obtain authorization from the patient's insurance. As a supervisor, I was called by the resident, who had found out, to his indignation, that the insurer would not cover the requested program. I worked with the resident on designing an ambulatory alternative. It quickly became clear that all the goals for the patient could be attained as well in an outpatient setting. To add background to the actual case, I referred the resident to the literature on effectiveness of treatment alternatives for chemical dependency (CD). The resident concluded that the insurance industry, in this case, had responded to the absence of compelling evidence that the treatment of substance abusers is less successful in an ambulatory setting than in an institution.[4]

Traditionally, residency training—like the bedside teaching of medical students—has occurred in the hospital inpatient setting. The requirements of the residency review committees for various specialties have begun to de-emphasize the amount of time allocated to inpatient training in response to a gradual shift toward ambulatory service delivery sites that predates the managed care movement. In the context of managed care, however, the relative ascendancy of outpatient care at the expense of hospital-based care has accelerated.

In psychiatry, the advent of managed care has led to a fundamental conceptual shift of our definition of the use of inpatient care. A large, venerable set of psychosocial literature about the therapeutic milieu and the rehabilitative functions of the psychiatric hospital has become largely obsolete.[5] Today's inpatient services are essentially crisis stabilization units with lengths of stay measured in days rather than weeks or months. Inpatient care is prescribed (and covered by third-party payers) only when a clinical decision maker believes that otherwise injury or death to a patient or others would result. In other words, the medical necessity criterion for hospitalization has become almost identical to customary commitment criteria.[6]

As a result, the projections for future use of inpatient resources have been downscaled. In one state's public mental health system, for instance, the estimate is that there will only be a need for ten inpatient beds for every 100,000 in the population.[7]

Managed care organizations (MCOs) competing on price for contracts can reduce their proposed rates by minimizing budgeted bed-days among the insured lives. Primarily they can do so by substituting intensive, easily accessed outpatient alternatives for hospital care. The example of CD treatment illustrates the trend. Traditional four-week inpatient programs are rapidly disappearing, and individually tailored outpatient programs are taking their place. The question of efficacy ("What works?") becomes critical, because renewal of contracts and long-term survival of managed care entities are tied to customer satisfaction and outcome measures.

The future design of psychiatric residency training programs will have to reflect these developments. Clearly, outpatient settings are becoming the primary training sites. Only nine out of forty-eight months of prescribed postgraduate training now must be devoted to inpatient psychiatry in order for a psychiatric residency training program to meet accreditation criteria.[8] Such a minimum requirement may be downscaled even further or eliminated altogether as the therapeutic specificity of the institutional setting becomes less relevant.

Changes in Curricular Content

The standard curriculum of psychiatric residency training will reflect the changes in the delivery system for behavioral health services. Quantified amounts of experience with defined treatment modes such as mood-stabilizing pharmacotherapy, cognitive therapy, and electroconvulsive therapy will be required, regardless of the site where such therapeutic services are delivered. It is probably safe to assume that the end of the conventional separation into outpatient years and inpatient years is on the horizon.

The cost-effectiveness of long-term psychotherapeutic treatments, including psychoanalysis and psychoanalytic psychotherapy, has been questioned in the market-oriented environment of managed care. Managed behavioral healthcare is not in the business of outlawing long-term psychotherapy, but of managing care. Managing care means the endeavor to maximize return on investment, which, in turn, implies optimization of the match between inputs of resources and outcomes for populations.[9]

This is a conceptually sound argument. In practice, though, we have found that traditional open-ended psychotherapy fares harder than it did in fee-for-service insurance arrangements or in direct contracting between patient and provider because quantifiable outcome measurements of such treatments are notoriously unreliable. In fact, the traditional model of psychodynamic therapies eschewed the notion of operationalized treatment targets, but was conceptualized as "open-ended." Without a measurable benefit in the numerator, however, any cost-per-unit of benefit is impossible to compute. By contrast, certain short-term verbal treatment protocols can be costed out in relation to beneficial effects. Thus, they lend themselves to inclusion in the benefit menus of managed care companies.

Obviously, there are implications for the therapeutic techniques that we teach our residents. The very paradigm of psychiatric care used to be psychodynamic therapy. Certain aspects of clinical psychiatry (and medicine in general) require a professional to be familiar with the psychodynamics of human behavior, developmental theory, and the concept of transference. Some educators will maintain that familiarization with psychological principles means that residents must take on patients for insight-oriented psychotherapy. I am not convinced that this is the case.

Closely monitored practical training in diagnostic interviewing may familiarize residents with skills to develop a dynamic formulation and initiate a biopsychosocial treatment plan. The principles of psychodynamic therapy have successfully been integrated in brief, focal psychotherapy and could presumably be conveyed experientially through that format.[10] If we accept the axiom that we must prepare residents for such a healthcare delivery environment as they are going to practice in, then it is our responsibility to orient our curricula toward treatments that patients will be able to purchase through their insurance plans.

The current residency training guidelines specify several psychosocial therapies that must be included in the clinical training experience. These therapies are psychodynamic psychotherapy, family therapy, group therapy, cognitive and behavior therapy, and crisis intervention. Preparation for the managed care environment would probably retain cognitive therapy in this catalog and emphasize focal dynamic therapy and time-limited group therapy, especially with a defined focus (such as a therapy group for patients with agoraphobia). There will also presumably be greater stress on a combination of psychosocial and biological treatments such as a dual-therapy protocol of behavioral therapy and pharmacological management for certain anxiety disorders. At the same time, didactics will continue to acquaint the resident in depth with the conceptual tenets of various schools of psychology, including classic psychoanalytic theory.

Utilization Management and Treatment Plans

Utilization management, which lies at the heart of all managed care, and the concept of treatment planning are important new content areas of residency curricula.

The principle of utilization management is optimization of the match between limited resources and the needs of a defined population of beneficiaries. At one point of service, in the course of a telephone conversation between a provider and a utilization manager, two worlds may clash: the one of the provider who is trained to maximize actual or perceived benefit for the individual patient in front of him or her, and the world of the utilization manager who is asked to allocate resources in such a way that the community of beneficiaries will maximize their aggregate utility.

Treatment plans, originally prescribed for hospital care settings, now also apply to outpatient settings. A treatment plan must include the definition of a problem, a measurable goal that serves as a criterion for termination of treatment, and a target date for accomplishment of the goal. Such a treatment plan permits a utilization manager proactive allocation of resources, which are estimated to support achievement of the identified goal. Increasingly, there are efforts under way to replace individualized treatment plans with problem-based prescribed clinical pathways. A particular constellation of factors (including a clinical diagnosis, chronicity, support systems, and comorbidity) serves as an input variable that triggers initiation of a preset sequence of interventions. The following comparison may illustrate the distance we have traveled.

In 1982, as a resident in my "outpatient year," I was assigned to write up an intake evaluation of a patient. I then had to present the evaluation to a diagnostic conference. The patient had come to the clinic complaining of chronic depressed mood, occasional suicidal ideation, and a profound sense of failure in his professional and private life.

My write-up consisted of a very detailed summary of the patient's developmental and social history. It culminated in a formulation that comprised a psychodynamic and a psychogenetic hypothesis, respectively; transference and countertransference predictions; a clinical diagnosis along the lines of the third edition of the *Diagnostic & Statistical Manual of Mental Disorders*; and a proposed therapy. The first four aspects of the formulation were thoroughly fleshed out, whereas the clinical diagnosis was a one-liner ("dysthymic disorder") and the treatment plan was summarized as "insight-oriented psychotherapy, once or twice weekly, long term."

Recently, I supervised a third-year resident who presented a new case to me that reminded me, clinically, of the patient I had to evaluate some thirteen years before. I asked the resident for a copy of her evaluation. Her write-up resembled the standard format of medical assessments. It summarized quite succinctly the patient's presenting complaint, history of present illness, past medical and psychiatric history (with particular emphasis on substance abuse), and social and family history. It ended in differential diagnosis for axes I and II and a tentative working diagnosis for all five axes. The affective features were quantified with rating scale scores.

After my discussion with the resident, she added a brief formulation ("Patient's failure in things he undertakes has become a firmly established self-fulfilling expectation") and a treatment plan. The plan connected presenting problems with specific interventions, quantified goals, and specific target dates. For instance, for the presenting problem "complaint of despondent mood with recurrent suicidal fantasies (Hamilton depression score 24)," the treatment interventions were "cognitive therapy, est. ten sessions, twice a week" and "paroxetine 20 mg/d for up to four months (may replace with nefazodone if side effects occur or paroxetine ineffective after four weeks)." The goal was a "decrease in Hamilton score by 50 percent."

In this case, the resident identified herself as the provider of both the psychotherapy and pharmacological services to the patient. Quite conceivably, she might have assigned the cognitive therapy component to a psychologist in her clinic and confined herself to the pharmacological management and the concluding evaluation of goal accomplishment.

Recognizing the role of utilization management and integrating it into the development of comprehensive care plans are educational challenges for residency training. Attention to treatment planning and the formulation of goals should contribute to the quality of care delivered by residents. Besides, they are vital preparatory steps in training residents for the managed care world where they will eventually practice.

Conventionally, treatment planning was seen as a nuisance associated with hospital practice. The head nurse insisted on treatment plans so that the hospital would be able to pass the next accreditation visit. The weary attitude of attending psychiatrists very probably colored the perception of their students. In a planned care environment, however, treatment plans have assumed critical importance. The key elements, outlined above, apply to outpatient care as much as to inpatient settings.

To the degree that residents become accustomed to a milieu of thoughtful allocation of treatment resources, they will also need to learn how to formulate treatment plans. This skill will have to be conveyed in a systematic manner, including preparatory didactics and experiential exposure. The challenge is to teach treatment planning in a constructive manner that transcends conventional defensive thinking. The treatment plan is no longer a way to comply with annoying regulations or to be prepared for hostile interrogation by a plaintiff's attorney one day. Rather, we introduce the treatment plan as an opportunity to map out a patient care strategy that permits both the providers and the patient (as well as external evaluators) to judge the effectiveness of our interventions.

Changes in Access to Patient Care

In the managed care environment, it is becoming more difficult for residents to find settings in which to train because of the cost of education and supervision and the perceived marketing problems of having trainees on a provider panel.

Teaching hospitals always had house staff providing services to their patients, and so did the clinics associated with the hospitals. Patients who could afford to go to "private hospitals" did so and avoided exposure to doctors in training. However, the boundary between public and private sectors is beginning to become blurred. Healthcare organizations with teaching missions have for many years reached out to insured patient populations in order to subsidize indigent care out of other patient care revenue ("cost shifting"). More recently, many states have aggressively pursued the option of enrolling Medicaid beneficiaries in MCOs. Resultant cost savings are then intended to open up Medicaid to larger groups, thus shrinking the number of uninsured people.

Managed care contracts often stipulate that only fully licensed providers may render services. The first and most important reason is financial. Residents must work under the supervision of attending physicians. They are therefore a net add-on cost, unless the cost of attending physicians can be reduced commensurately.

The second reason concerns product marketing: the prospect of being treated by a resident is likely to be perceived as indicative of lower quality of care, sometimes equated with "indigent care." In areas of high MCO market penetration, the combination of both factors makes it quite difficult for teaching institutions to integrate their residents and fellows in the very areas of their clinical operations that have the greatest growth potential.

Changes in Funding

There are various ways to address the dilemma. We have found it possible to sell the participation of residents as members of a provider panel by making explicit, in quantitative and measurable terms, the relationship between a resident and his or her attending physician. The resident may be seen as a highly qualified psychiatrist-extender. The message is that the involvement of residents presents a provider-set with higher physician density than competing panels.

Closely related to this approach is a carefully designed pricing method. The total cost in terms of charge for member per month (under capitation) or for a unit of service (under pure or modified fee-for-service terms) must not exceed that of an alternative plan that offers attending psychiatrists with nonphysician extenders in its provider mix. I have managed to change clinical faculty members' job descriptions in such a way that the provision of clinical duties is part of their academic position. The paycheck they receive is composed of traditionally sourced reimbursement for teaching students and clinical revenue that covers both the faculty members' salary and the resident stipend to the degree that both are related to servicing patients in the MCO clinic.

As some states mandate inclusion of medical schools in the provider panels for managed Medicaid contracts, the situation may become easier. In order to be accredited by the Joint Commission for Accreditation of Healthcare Organizations, for example, MCOs must not systematically discriminate between the insured lives they serve. If a particular protocol involving residents applies to an MCO's Medicaid patients, it would be problematic to argue that non-Medicaid patients are entitled to a different protocol.

The option of disregarding MCOs that question the introduction of residents is shortsighted. For the time being, there may still be enough alternatives from the fee-for-service sector, especially Medicare. Several historical examples are available, however, to demonstrate the predictable dynamics of market penetration once the managed care movement has established a foothold in a geographical area. Training institutions that fail to engage the problem proactively are likely to dry up financially and, before long, lose access to patients.

The Importance of Licensing Residents

In order to fit in the world of managed care, residents must be licensed. This necessity requires training directors to be more vigilant than ever in the recruitment stages. International medical graduates in particular must clearly qualify for a permanent state medical license before they can be signed on. Most states require at least one year of medical practice before they issue a license. This internship year can generally be managed through issuance of institutional, restricted licenses. During the following years of training, however, the ability to provide a cadre of fully licensed physicians as a complement of the provider panel is an asset that should not be underestimated.

Funding Issues in Resident Education

House staff have traditionally occupied an ambiguous niche in the professional employment world. They are not employees of a healthcare institution, regular students, or members of the faculty or medical staff. The ambiguity is reflected in funding arrangements. Residents receive stipends rather than salaries. Their pay is usually based on a variety of sources. Hospitals are reimbursed by the Health Care Financing Administration for medical education expenses by a surcharge to their Medicare reimbursement for hospital services and use these funds to support residents and residency teaching activities. The Department of Veterans' Affairs and, to varying degrees, departments of mental health at the state level fund residents' stipends. The shared motivation is an interest in preparing a cadre of well-trained future physicians who may become career professionals within the system that underwrote part of their training.

MCOs often have a more short-term outlook. Contracts are awarded or denied based on the price to be entered into the vendor's budget for the next year. If training adds cost, the risk of unsuccessfully bidding is greater. MCOs are therefore averse to considering training if it presents itself as an added cost. In some cases, university training centers have a strong enough market position in terms of available manpower, expertise, and local reputation that MCOs are willing to swallow some add-on costs of training.

In other instances, state legislative action can mandate that MCOs must include university practices and their trainees on their panels in order to be eligible for bidding on Medicaid contracts. Some programs may be able to find alternative funding sources, such as the state, or will rely, for the time being, on cost shifting— until the degree of penetration of the local market by managed care makes that tactic impossible. Some programs will downsize their residency classes, others may close.

Trends Within the Profession

The market-driven dynamics shaping the design of providers' products in the managed care environment have again raised the question of whether it takes a medical degree to administer psychotherapy. Generally, the answer has been negative. Whether they are staff models or networks, groups of providers selling behavioral healthcare services have been able to deliver services for populations of insured lives at physician-consumer ratios that are much lower than the current ratios of doctors per thousand of population or than the current density of psychiatrists in the United States. The role of psychiatrists is increasingly being defined as the assessment of patients (initial diagnostic evaluation and reassessment in refractory cases) and as psychopharmacologic consultation.

The psychiatrist in an MCO functions as a professional resource person in a team. He or she may or may not be the leader of the team, but adds, in any case, unique skills and competencies that are unlikely to be available from other professionals. The comprehensive differential diagnostic evaluation is one such valued expertise. In a service delivery philosophy that assesses efficacy on the basis of outcomes for populations served (rather than individually), this competency, which comes at a price, is not a routine requirement of care, but factored in as a resource to be mobilized in selected cases.

The resident who is trained for a role in such a system must learn how to actively define the psychiatrist's contribution to the patient care plan, how to respond to consultation questions, and how to communicate effectively with other professionals. The actual psychosocial management is more and more the domain of professionals who are not psychiatrists: licensed social workers, nurses at the master's degree level, clinical psychologists, and primary care physicians all play their roles, as do case managers with a variety of backgrounds.

Extrapolation of recent ratios in managed care organizations to the United States as a whole would predict a need for only about 10,000 psychiatrists in the country.[11] In the late 1980s, about 35,000 U.S. physicians classified themselves as psychiatrists.[12] As of April 1995, the American Psychiatric Association counted 39,790 members.[13] I doubt that the simple extrapolation from current managed care staffing patterns is an accurate preview of future manpower needs, because the more service-intensive chronic mentally ill are largely excluded from current arrangements, but would become a factor in a universally managed healthcare delivery environment. However, there will probably be a decreased need for psychiatrists in the future healthcare market, just as there will be less need for many other specialties.

The number of graduates of U.S. medical schools who were starting residency training in psychiatry was 4,641 in 1991, but only 3,866 in 1994.[14] That trend of declining enrollment of American medical graduates in psychiatric residency programs probably will continue. There have been reciprocal trends in family medicine and general internal medicine, so some residency program directors have elected to design combined psychiatry-primary care courses. At the end of such training, graduates will be able to take board examinations in both psychiatry and the primary care specialty. In this way, they would preserve potential marketability as primary care physicians, but could use their expertise in mental illness in their practices. A program offering such double-board training could conceivably buck the trend of the shrinking attraction of psychiatric residency training.

—⁓—

A psychiatrist is a physician who has been trained to diagnose and treat mental disorders. I see no reason to revise this global definition substantially. The trends that operate on the profession and its training programs, however, are shifting the relative weights of various components covered by the definition. A key function is the one that other medical specialists have developed for a long time: today's psychiatrists are increasingly consultants to other professionals, especially primary care physicians. They also are likely to remain the providers of choice in the comprehensive care for individuals with severe chronic mental illness. The treatment for individuals with less crippling problems will be the domain of other mental health professionals. Wellness enhancement and lifestyle medicine (such as programs to quit smoking and groups to revitalize marriages) are developing markets. The psychiatrist of the future ought to ensure that our profession remains involved, screening clients who want this kind of help, designing treatment plans, and being ready for consultation when needed.

Notes

1. Lazarus, A. (1995). An annotated bibliography in managed care for psychiatric residents and faculty. *Academic Psychiatry, 19,* 65–73.
2. American Medical Association. (1995). *Graduate medical education 1995–1996.* Chicago: American Medical Association, pp. 218–238.
3. Hillard, J. R., Zitek, B., & Thienhaus, O. J. (1994). Residency training in emergency psychiatry: Changes between 1980 and 1990. *Academic Psychiatry, 17,* 125–129.
4. Hayashida, M., Alterman, A. I., & Associates. (1989). Comparative effectiveness and cost of inpatient and outpatient detoxification of patients with mild to moderate alcohol with-

drawal syndrome. *New England Journal of Medicine, 320,* 358–365.

5. Jones, M. (1953). *The therapeutic community.* New Haven, CT: Yale University Press.
6. Thienhaus, O. J., & Schuster, J. M. (1995). Utilization management and other administrative issues for the inpatient psychiatrist. In O. J. Thienhaus (Ed.), *Manual of clinical hospital psychiatry* (pp. 182–206). Washington, DC: American Psychiatric Press.
7. Ohio Department of Mental Health. (1993). *The future of inpatient mental health services in Ohio.* Columbus, OH: Ohio Department of Mental Health.
8. *Graduate medical education 1995–1996,* pp. 218–238.
9. Sabin, J. E., & Borus, J. F. (1992). Mental health teaching and research in managed care. In J. L. Feldman & R. J. Fitzpatrick (Eds.), *Managed mental health care: Administrative and clinical issues* (pp. 185–199). Washington, DC: American Psychiatric Press.
10. Sifneos, P. E. (1984). The current status of short-term dynamic psychotherapy. *American Journal of Psychotherapy, 38,* 472–483.
11. Kronick, R., Goodman, D. C., & Associates. (1993). The marketplace in health care reform. *New England Journal of Medicine, 328,* 148–152.
12. Dial, T. H., Tebbutt, R., & Associates. (1990). Human resources in mental health. In R. W. Manderscheid & M. A. Sonnenschein (Eds.), *Mental Health United States 1990. U.S. Department of Health and Human Services Publ. No. (ADM) 90–1708* (pp. 196–206). Washington, DC: Government Printing Office.
13. Sharfstein, S. S. (1995). Report of the secretary. *American Journal of Psychiatry, 152,* 1541–1542.
14. American Psychiatric Association. (1995). *1994–1995 Resident Census Data.* Washington, DC: American Psychiatric Association, Table 7.

Chapter Three

Creating the New Psychiatric Residency

Marcia Kaplan

I am the medical director of both a multidisciplinary group practice and a managed care corporation affiliated with the department of psychiatry at the University of Cincinnati. The group practice, University Psychiatric Services (UPS), was created in 1983 to provide outpatient services on a contractual basis. It functions with a core staff of practitioners in a "private practice" setting. Triage and initial assessments are done by experienced social workers who, with my review, refer patients to the group of psychiatrists, psychologists, and social workers. Most patients are treated in a short-term format.

University Managed Care, Inc. (UMC) was created in 1990 to provide services to capitated and point-of-service populations. It also provides utilization management services. UMC uses UPS as a major, but not exclusive provider of services to its enrollees. UMC currently is capitated for 35,000 covered lives.

The principles of managed care make a good deal of sense to me, and although I am acutely aware of its limitations, I am excited about the positive changes in practice standards that have resulted. My past experiences in my psychiatry residency and as a resident in neurology have convinced me that psychodynamic understanding combined with an appreciation for neurobiology and psychopharmacology enable one to do high-quality work in a managed care environment, or any environment, without sacrificing career satisfaction. I hope to take part in preparing psychodynamically sensitive and pharmacologically up-to-date psychiatrists who benefit patients as much as payers.

A New Curriculum

There is an ongoing shift away from long-term, insight-oriented psychotherapy as the model for outpatient treatment and toward a more pragmatic, outcome-oriented, supportive approach.[1] The following are elements of this shift that should be addressed.

Emphasis on Short-Term Treatment

In the academic community, there is still a bias that favors long-term approaches to psychotherapy, although this preference is based more on personal experience than on controlled studies. Payers, on the other hand, favor—and fund—short-term, outcome-oriented approaches in the absence of data supporting the efficacy of insight-oriented care. In fact, since well before the advent of managed care, the most common length of stay in psychotherapy has been fewer than eight sessions.[2] Therefore, it makes sense to teach residents to use a short-term format, moving to more intensive or differently focused treatments only if brief treatment fails. This is a departure from the assumption of the past few decades that all patients should be offered long-term treatment until proven otherwise.

Earlier Use of Medication

Medication is often the fastest and most effective treatment option. Greater exposure in the popular media and the increasing provision of prescriptions for psychotherapeutic drugs by primary care physicians have made patients more sophisticated about medications when they enter treatment. Traditional psychoanalytically informed training stressed evaluating new patients for response to initial psychotherapeutic interventions before considering use of medication and warned that symptom relief with medication might encourage patients to leave treatment prematurely. This concern could only be considered a problem when the relationship between the patient and the psychiatrist was seen as timeless, ongoing, and financially supportable.

For patients with limited resources, especially those with disabling symptoms and clear-cut diagnoses, medication should be offered as early as the initial interview. Medication does not interfere with psychotherapy; in my experience, significantly depressed patients are better able to make use of psychotherapy once their depression has lifted and concentration has been restored. The argument that relieving symptoms may remove the patient's motivation for psychotherapy also overlooks the fact that many patients want symptom relief rather than insight.

Psychiatrists working in multidisciplinary group practices, community outpatient clinics, or health maintenance organization (HMO) settings will frequently see a high volume of patients for medication management only. Some of these patients are seeing non-M.D. therapists for psychotherapy, some have terminated an episode of psychotherapy, and some have no interest in psychotherapy. There is strong evidence supporting the long-term use of medication for many patients, particularly those with recurrent or chronic illness.[3] The psychiatrist may serve an important supportive function for some patients even if seen only once or twice per year, whereas other patients will do well with internists or family doctors prescribing a successful regimen.

Patients who are stable may be seen infrequently, and I find brief telephone contact to be an adequate or even optimal between-visit follow-up for many patients. Mental health benefits allowing a fixed number of sessions may not differentiate between a full psychotherapy session and a fifteen-minute medication follow-up visit. Psychiatrists who insist on frequent medication checks with reasonably stable patients who are in psychotherapy with others may be preempting or competing with the psychotherapist.

As psychiatry residents are increasingly interacting with non-M.D. trainees, training directors and supervisors must be attuned to the potential for inadequate communication or struggles over "turf." These issues will quickly surface in practice settings if they have not been brought into focus during residency. Training conferences that include residents with psychology and social work trainees will help clarify the differences in proficiencies and focus of each profession and will set a precedent for open discussion of how clinical problems are approached. Supervisors' involvement may be the most appropriate conduit for dealing with struggles arising between particular trainees.

Emphasis on Support over Insight

Supportive psychotherapy has traditionally been viewed as a second-class treatment reserved only for low-functioning patients who are incapable of insight. In fact, insight-oriented treatment is often helpful because of its supportive aspects: regular contact with a helpful and empathic person who offers a model for more effective problem solving and less self-criticism. Supportive treatment can be concrete or psychodynamically oriented, according to the patient's needs. Psychodynamically oriented supportive treatment should be considered the optimal treatment for the "average" out-patient.[4]

Residents should be encouraged to engage in some long-term or (given the limitations of residency) ongoing insight-oriented treatment with appropriate patients. Residents must learn the indications for supportive as opposed to insight-oriented treatment, so they can offer a more intensive approach only to patients likely to benefit from it.

A female senior resident working on a psychobiology outpatient clinic rotation recommended twice weekly therapy to a divorced male office manager who presented with intense depression and angry outbursts with coworkers. This behavior threatened his job. She initiated treatment of the patient with an antidepressant, and engaged him in an exploratory process of remembering his troubled childhood. He reported frightening nightmares that worsened as the treatment went on. He became more symptomatic, and lithium and a benzodiazepine were added. The resident was not presenting the case to a psychotherapy supervisor, so the psychopharmacology supervisor did not recognize that the patient's worsening was connected to the intensive psychotherapy. The patient became suicidal and required hospitalization, at which point the resident presented the case to her psychotherapy supervisor. They agreed that though the patient seemed in some ways to have adequate ego strengths to benefit from insight-oriented psychotherapy, he had severe psychopathology resulting from traumatic childhood experience and was unable to tolerate the regression that resulted from the twice-weekly sessions. After discharge, he was seen every two weeks, with significant stabilization and eventual improvement.

Varied Treatment Modalities

Individual psychotherapy is often effective for adjustment disorders, but different patient populations may respond better to treatments focused on specific symptoms. For example, depressed patients may be ideal candidates for cognitive therapy, which may be started in either inpatient or outpatient settings, and may be computer-assisted.[5] Obsessive-compulsive or phobic patients, however, may be best treated with behavioral desensitization to the feared situation.[6] Impulsive, suicidal borderline patients have improved significantly with dialectical-behavioral treatment.[7] Patients with recurrent interpersonal problems may benefit most from solution-focused therapy and patients with personality disorders may be best treated in group settings where they can develop improved social skills and obtain peer support.[8] Patients suffering from posttraumatic stress disorders may need combined individual, medication, and group treatment. They also may be candidates for eye movement reprocessing.[9] Still other patients may get great benefit from educational groups focused on specific diagnoses, such as attention-deficit disorder, panic disorder, or depression, or on specific topics such as parenting, stress management, or conflict resolution. Community resources such as women's centers, twelve-step programs, gay-lesbian groups, and weight-loss programs may be important adjuncts to psychotherapy. It is therefore crucial that trainees be versed in a wide variety of therapies.

Focus on Outcomes

The wide differences in technique, skill, and experience of therapists, the lack of a "placebo" treatment, long length of treatment, confidentiality issues, and other factors have always made the efficacy of psychotherapy difficult to assess.[10] Traditional teaching all but ignored the issue of outcome, stressing instead the unique nature of each patient-therapist dyad, and the importance of gaining insight rather than functional improvement. Residents need exposure to the many standardized tests available for making accurate diagnoses and tracking progress. These tests include pretreatment and posttreatment surveys of patient functioning such as the Brief Symptom Inventory; the SF-36; the Global Assessment Scale; the Progress Evaluation Scale, and others that allow for standardized evaluation of the outcome of treatment, even if the treatment itself is not standardized.[11] There are many questionnaires designed for rating specific conditions or making standard diagnoses. These tools include the Beck Depression Inventory, the Hamilton Depression Rating Scale, the Yale-Brown Obsessive-Compulsive Scale, the Michigan Alcoholism Screening Test, and the Structured Clinical Interview for DSM-IV.[12]

New Ethical Issues

Managed care, which by definition involves review of the interaction between doctor and patient, has ushered in a new set of ethical issues, in addition to traditional concerns about confidentiality and boundaries violations. Though third parties have long been involved in the interaction between psychiatrist and patient, never before has this meant the review of clinical data to determine what treatment and which clinician will be covered. Furthermore, the emphasis on short-term and pharmacological treatment may prevent trainees from learning firsthand about the boundary issues raised by intensive therapies.

Confidentiality

Most managed care plans require telephone "triage" interviews with utilization management personnel who establish patient profiles in a computerized medical information system and determine allowed benefits. Many patients are surprised at being asked for details about their reasons for seeking treatment and object to disclosing personal information to an insurance functionary. In my experience, the psychiatrist can be quite helpful in training utilization personnel to elicit information in a nonthreatening manner and to reassure patients about the reasons for this procedure and its confidentiality. Although psychiatrists are not involved in this process of securing access to treatment, it is important that they know what patients may experience before getting to their offices. This knowledge is equally important for residents who see clinic patients after an intake process has taken place.

Denials of Treatment

Enrollees in managed care plans frequently believe (and may be led to believe by employee benefits counselors) that they are entitled to a fixed yearly number of psychotherapy sessions. In fact, many contracts stipulate a maximum number of sessions available for the treatment of acute crises that meet criteria for medical necessity. In other words, ongoing psychotherapy for lifelong neurotic conflicts that makes use of the full number of allotted sessions year after year is not a covered benefit. At UMC we give careful consideration to this problem and educate staff therapists to differentiate between ongoing treatment that may be desirable but not covered and supportive treatment that limits regression and maximizes functioning. I have found that some insurers make precipitous denials once a treatment process is under way. Residents need to have specific training about the preparation of requests for treatment authorization and when to appeal decisions. It is important to define implications of language used in writing requests; for instance, vagueness about the focus of psychotherapy may be interpreted as the psychiatrist's intent to conduct an open-ended psychoanalytic psychotherapy.

A resident began weekly sessions with a working divorced mother with a history of alcoholism in remission and abusive relationships with men. The patient was given to moodiness that interfered with her capacity to care for her children and function at work. Extensive medication trials did not adequately control her depression and mood instability.

The patient's HMO policy allowed a maximum of twenty session per year; sixteen were approved for the first calendar year, and sixteen for the following year. Over the course of the thirty-two sessions, she stabilized to the extent that she was able to leave a destructive relationship and gain a promotion at work. The resident requested more sessions "to help patient work through childhood traumatic experience that leads to depression and hopelessness," and was surprised when further treatment was denied, ostensibly because "psychotherapy for purpose of personality change" was not covered by her HMO.

The supervisor suggested appealing the decision with the HMO medical director. He formulated the case as one of high severity that would benefit from less frequent supportive sessions for maintenance of remission, thus preventing more costly crisis intervention in the future. The HMO medical director overturned the decision, allowing sessions on a once-monthly basis.

Boundary Issues

There should be an ever-present focus on the maintenance of clear boundaries by the psychiatrist. Psychotherapists are at risk for allowing boundary violations if they are professionally, emotionally, or socially isolated. Especially in today's climate with an emphasis on brief and pharmacological treatments, residents should receive training in traditional psychoanalytic principles such as therapeutic alliance, transference, countertransference, resistance, regression, not only in a didactic format, but in case discussions and supervision. These principles are operative no matter what the scope of contact with patients. Even with shorter treatments and less intensive treatment relationships, the psychiatrist may be consulted for many "episodes" of treatment by a given patient. There is an enormous differential of power between therapist and patient, and this should be respected even after the treatment relationship has ended.

The New Residency

Current-day residency training was designed to reflect the realities of practice before the advent of managed care. As the standards of practice change, residency programs must begin to reflect the new practice environment that graduates will enter.

Residency Should Resemble Practice

Long-term, insight-oriented psychotherapy has been the accepted model of optimal psychiatric practice for many decades, and residency has been designed to prepare trainees for a career primarily as psychotherapists. It was once reasonable to expect that most graduates could make comfortable incomes as solo private practitioners in urban areas. Solo practice might include inpatient work, either in a rotation with other psychiatrists on the hospital staff or with one's own patients. More experienced, highly trained psychiatrists were generally able to confine their practice to outpatients in psychoanalytic psychotherapy.[13]

Today, however, new graduates will be more likely to enter group practices or community agencies where they may be paid a salary rather than fee-for-service compensation. They will certainly face more involvement with third-party managers and reviewers, whether in private practice or as managed care organization staff members. The public sector is increasingly managed, so community mental health centers and other state-and county-subsidized agencies may be "carved out" to have services provided or administered by for-profit companies. Inpatient treatment will continue to be limited to those who cannot be treated in a less restrictive environment. Patients are likely to be referred for medication management only, with concurrent assignments to non-M.D. psychotherapists if psychotherapy is considered necessary.

Training must begin to reflect these changes and help prepare graduates not only to cope, but to thrive as psychiatrists. Programs currently overemphasize inpatient treatment, do not provide for adequate follow-up of patients discharged after brief inpatient or outpatient interventions, do not provide enough exposure to community resources, promote long-term psychotherapy or eliminate psychotherapy training as irrelevant, and do not integrate biological and psychodynamic approaches. Residents cannot afford to enter the marketplace with a narrow range of competence.

Incorporating Administrative Issues

In my experience as a resident, an attending inpatient psychiatrist, a private practitioner, and a managed care medical director, I have thought of administrative issues as far less interesting than the actual work of interviewing, diagnosing, and treating psychiatric illness. However, I have come to see the administrative as increasingly relevant to the clinical, not only because one cannot proceed without the other, but because benefit limits have led me to careful consideration of what works and what doesn't. Residents will understandably be less attuned to authorizing treatment than to learning how to do it, but experience with supervisors can have an enormous effect on attitudes.

Most faculty in academic departments of psychiatry trained before the advent of managed care and with vastly different assumptions about practice. Only ten years ago, the standard for all outpatient treatment was open-ended and insight-oriented. Inpatient treatment was often covered more generously than outpatient sessions, and hospital admissions were seen as opportunities for extended diagnostic evaluations. Interaction with third-party payers was limited to submitting a diagnosis code. Therefore, mid-level and senior faculty may feel betrayed by what they perceive to be a threat to their professional autonomy when they are asked to provide information to reviewers.

Attending psychiatrists may communicate contempt for utilization reviewers asking for information about medical necessity, overtly or covertly. Residents who have not been engaged in a reasoned discussion of the various treatment alternatives for a given patient and the reasons for choosing a particular approach are at a disadvantage if they are expected, as "low man on the totem pole," to discuss details of a case with a reviewer. Attending physicians who recognize this aspect of inpatient work as an opportunity to discuss a biopsychosociofiscal formulation will not only prepare the resident to discuss the case intelligently with a reviewer, but will sharpen his or her skills at formulation.[14]

Many training programs will include outpatient training sites with institutionally imposed limitations on the scope and duration of treatment. Residents should be involved in the authorization process from the beginning of their work with patients. The community mental health center that serves as the major outpatient training site for University of Cincinnati psychiatry residents has instituted a managed care model. In this model, patients are given a twelve-session limit, which can be extended if the resident makes a written request for more sessions, documenting medical necessity and a treatment plan. Residents attend a weekly multidisciplinary conference staffed by a faculty psychiatrist and a staff social worker where new cases are presented and discussed. Residents, psychology interns, and social work students hear about one another's work and outlook, thus fostering greater capacity for collaboration in the future.

Ideally, residents would also have an opportunity to work with utilization reviewers or medical directors who make treatment authorization decisions. Various university training programs with affiliated MCOs have offered electives for residents to work with managed care staff. There are also collaborative efforts being forged between MCOs and residency programs to allow residents to work in managed care practices and learn about the industry. University-affiliated clinical programs, whether inpatient or outpatient, should include a quality improvement process that residents can be involved in.

Shifting the Training Sequence

Residency training traditionally begins on the inpatient unit, where trainees learn to recognize symptoms and syndromes, to use medication and assess results, and to involve family members in developing a biopsychosocial treatment plan. Additionally, residents begin to understand group dynamics both among patients on the unit and in their own interactions with the treatment team. These goals were attainable when average stays were two weeks or more, but are increasingly difficult to accomplish as the inpatient unit comes to resemble an intensive care unit.[15] Residents may not get to know patients well enough to feel involved with them, may not see the full effects of the medications they prescribe, and may not experience the cohesive group process of the traditional inpatient milieu.

As psychiatry becomes more "medical," with advances in the physiology, pharmacology, and genetics of psychiatric illness, and as psychiatry becomes more "primary care," there is good reason to increase trainees' exposure to internal medicine and neurology. Adding a full year of medicine and neurology to the training sequence would not only better prepare residents intellectually, but would also enable them to feel like "real doctors" who are confident among their medical peers.

Given the fast pace and high intensity of the inpatient unit, it may make more sense to begin residents in an outpatient setting where they can work closely with an attending psychiatrist. Outpatients are more likely to be stable enough to allow for gathering of data, diagnosis, and treatment that can be followed over a period of time, ideally the length of the residency. The emergency service also gives the resident an opportunity to interview patients with attending supervision on site. After gaining a measure of proficiency in conducting an interview, recognizing syndromes, and formulating a diagnosis and treatment plan, the resident would be prepared to enter the more pressured inpatient environment. Inpatient assignments should include time to follow patients in partial programs that may serve as "step-down units" after discharge.

Training for New Practice Settings

With non-M.D. therapists providing psychotherapy and primary care physicians increasingly prescribing psychotropic medication, fewer psychiatrists will be supported in densely populated urban areas.[16] Graduates will need to consider working in underserved areas, whether suburban or rural. Training programs can introduce residents to practice settings such as forensic clinics, rural mental health services, or family practice offices. Careful planning and sensitivity to staff attitudes on the part of faculty setting up such training sites can ensure successful training experiences and can lead to more graduates entering these areas.[17]

Incorporating Treatment Teams

As an alternative to the current sequence of rotations in which residents move from one site to the next, encountering different patient populations in each setting, several psychiatric educators have suggested moving to the use of treatment teams or firms, much like the vertically organized groups used in medical and surgical training.[18] These groups would include an attending faculty psychiatrist, a faculty psychologist, a social worker or case manager for inpatients, a senior resident, a junior resident, medical students, and psychology and social work interns. Each team would cover a variety of functions, including emergency service, inpatient unit, consultation-liaison, and outpatient clinic. They would pick up new cases in a rotation with other teams. Residents would switch teams in six- or nine-month intervals.

The advantage of the team approach includes the exposure of residents to different training sites repeatedly over the course of their training and in changing roles as they gain professional maturity. The disadvantage, for which the team approach has been criticized in Britain, where it is in operation, is the distance of trainees from experienced attending physicians, with most of the teaching done by trainees one level up. The team experience is service-oriented, rather than focused on educational needs. It will be important to learn from the experience of programs such as those at the University of Washington and Dartmouth University, which have instituted the team system.

Using Case Conferences

Case conferences are a time-honored method of bringing theoretical principles to life and allowing for questions and discussion about the dilemmas posed and choices made in carrying out diagnosis and treatment. This is a particularly valuable format for helping residents think about dealing with limited resources and contrasting the needs of the individual with the needs of the population. Supervisors must themselves feel comfortable with these issues and capable of presenting a range of theories, styles, and techniques. Supervisors should be oriented to the pressures residents feel to treat a high volume of patients in a short-term format, if the supervisors themselves do not face these pressures. It is especially helpful for residents to realize that there is more than one correct approach to a patient, and that pragmatic concerns must enter into the decision about the treatment chosen.

—∿—

Managed care has led to real changes in the practice patterns of psychiatrists, with a new emphasis on cost-effectiveness and out-come of treatment. This shift necessarily means a change in the outlook and responsibilities of currently practicing psychiatrists, but can and should be part of the training of future practitioners. Today's graduating psychiatrists are entering a profession that is changing and will continue to evolve. Adapting residency training curricula to the realities of practice in the twenty-first century will enable new graduates to enter the managed care marketplace with confidence and the right skills for the job.

Notes

1. Yager, J., & Robinowitz, C. (1996). Psychiatry and psychiatric practice in the year 2020. In L. J. Dickstein, J. M. Oldham, & M. B. Riba (Eds.), *Annual Review of Psychiatry*, vol. 15. Washington, DC: American Psychiatric Press.
2. Garfield, S. L. (1986). Research on client variables in psychotherapy. In S. L. Garfield & A. E. Bergin (Eds.), *Handbook of psychotherapy and behavior change*. New York: Wiley.
3. Consensus Development Panel. (1985). Mood disorders: Pharmacologic prevention of recurrences (NIMH/NIH Consensus Development Conference Statement). *American Journal of Psychiatry, 142*, 469–476.
4. Rockland, L. H. (1989). *Supportive therapy: A psychodynamic approach*. New York: Basic Books.
5. Wright, J. H., & Beck, A. T. (1994). Cognitive therapy. In R. E. Hales, S. C. Yudofsky, & J. A. Talbott (Eds.), *The American*

Psychiatric Press textbook of psychiatry (2nd ed.). Washington, DC: American Psychiatric Press.

6. Foa, E. B., & Wilson, R. (1991). *Stop obsessing!* New York: Bantam Books.

7. Linehan, M. M. (1993). *Cognitive-behavioral treatment of borderline personality disorder.* New York: Guilford Press.

8. deShazer, S. (1988). *Clues: Investigating solutions in brief therapy.* New York: Norton.

9. Shapiro, F. (1995). *Eye movement desensitization and reprocessing: Basic principles, protocols, and procedures.* New York: Guilford Press.

10. Lambert, M. J., Shapiro, D. A., & Bergin, A. E. (1986). The effectiveness of psychotherapy. In S. L. Garfield & A. E. Bergin (Eds.), *Handbook of psychotherapy and behavior change.* New York: Wiley.

11. Derogatis, L. (1985). *Brief symptom inventory.* Minneapolis: National Computer Systems; Ware, J. E., & Sherbourne, C. D. (1991). The SF-36 short form health status survey I: conceptual framework and item selection. Boston: New England Medical Centers Hospital, International Resource Center for Health Care Assessment; Endicott, J., Spitzer, R., Fleiss, J., & Cohen, J. (1976). The global assessment scale. *Archives of General Psychiatry, 33,* 766–771; Ihilebich, D., & Gleser, G. C. (1982). *Evaluating mental health programs: The Progress Evaluation Scale.* Lexington, MA: Lexington Books.

12. Beck, A. T., Ward, C. H., Mendelson, M., Mock, J., & Erbaugh, J. (1961). An inventory for measuring depression. *Archives of General Psychiatry, 4,* 561–571; Hamilton, M. (1967). Development of a rating scale for primary depressive illness. *British Journal of Social and Clinical Psychology, 6,* 278–296; Goodman, W. K., Price, L. H., Rasmussen, S. A., Mazure, C., et al. (1989). The Yale-Brown obsessive-compulsive scale: I. Development, use and reliability. *Archives of General Psychiatry, 46,* 1006–1011; Selzer, M. L., Vinokur, A., & van Rooijen, L. A. (1975). A self-administered short Michigan

alcoholism screening test (SMAST). *Journal of Studies on Alcohol, 36,* 117; Spitzer, R. L., Williams, J. B., Gibbon, M., et al. (1994). *Structured clinical interview for DSM-IV (SCID).* New York: Biometric Research Department, New York State Psychiatric Institute.

13. Shore, M. F., & Beigel, A. (1996). The challenges posed by managed behavioral health care. *New England Journal of Medicine, 334* (2), 116–118.

14. Lewis, J. M., & Blotcky, M. J. (1993). Living and learning with managed care. *Academic Psychiatry, 17,* 186–193.

15. Beresin, E. V. (1995, August). Curricula for new training models. In S. A. Talbott, J. W. Lomax, E. V. Beresin, C. H. L. Chin, F. Guggenheim, P. C. Mohl, & A. Tasman (Eds.), *Proceedings of an American Association of Chairmen of Departments of Psychiatry Conference.* Baltimore, August 15–17, 1995.

16. Weiner, J. P. (1994). Forecasting the effects of health reform on US physician workforce requirement. *Journal of the American Medical Association, 272,* 222–233.

17. Santos, A. B., Ballenger, J. C., Bevilacqua, J. J., Zealberg, J. J., Hiers, T. G., MacLeod-Bryant, S., Deci, P. A., & Rames, L. J. (1994). A community-based public-academic liaison program. *American Journal of Psychiatry, 151,* 1181–1187.

18. Smith, C. S. (1995). The impact of an ambulatory firm system on quality and continuity of care. *Medical Care, 33,* 221–226.

Chapter Four

Managed Care's Impact on Graduate Psychology Training Programs

David B. Shaw

Managed care has been looming on my horizon since I began my career as a professional psychologist. At that time, I worked for the Veterans Administration (VA), where the talk was of diagnosis-related groups (DRGs), resource allocation models (RAMs), and utilization review (UR). In spite of all this talk, I saw very little happening that I would now consider to have seriously affected the patient care models being used. Patients were still routinely inhabiting the psychiatric wards for relatively long stays (twenty-one to twenty-eight days). Patients who presented difficult diagnostic dilemmas were being admitted for observation and evaluation, sometimes without regard to level of distress or impairment.

Meanwhile, back at the graduate schools, the same kind of pattern was occurring. We knew that changes were coming in our models of treatment, but the reality of those changes could easily be ignored in our daily practice because most major metropolitan areas were still dominated by traditional models of care and insurance coverage. While I have administered psychology internship training, participated in a clinical training committee at a VA consortium, and now serve as a training director at a private tertiary care hospital, I have observed that very little changed in our models of training until the past few years. This lethargic response to the arrival of managed care occurred in spite of some early predictions that our methods of care delivery would be changing, and that the kind of training that we must do in order to adapt to new patient care models would need to be changing as well.[1]

Consequences of Managed Care

I realized some of the unexpected consequences for training programs early on in my exposure to managed care. I had always taken for granted that somehow the subsidization of training of mental healthcare providers would be shared by the third-party payers under a managed care system as it had in the past. At the VA, this meant that the federal government would provide training stipends for psychology interns as it had for almost fifty years. In the private sector, our assumption was that health insurance companies would continue to allow psychology trainees to provide care under the direct supervision of licensed psychologists.

The surprise came when our department first started to apply to be providers to managed care and I innocently asked how we should document care that was provided by a psychology intern under our supervision. I was told that interns would not be allowed to provide the care under that managed care contract. This was the first of many similar shocks that came about as we saw our local healthcare market transforming to managed care. Indeed, other managed care companies were requiring similar restrictions on care provided by trainees and other nonlicensed providers.

Concurrently, our internship program noticed an increasing number of applicants who did not secure training sites on internship selection day. Likewise, it was becoming more difficult for our interns to find their first postdoctoral positions as they completed their training. Traditional opportunities that were available at facilities like our hospital were dwindling as we began to reduce our staff size to accommodate significant reductions in reimbursement rates from managed care. Furthermore, the same supervision issues facing predoctoral internships were also affecting the employment of nonlicensed postdoctoral-level providers: i.e., the managed care companies would not reimburse for care provided by those who had not met the companies' minimum qualifications and been certified as providers on their panels.

Retooling for the Managed Care Era

We are making headway at regaining some of the training ground lost when managed care first surfaced in our area, but this problem calls into question our attitudes and planning as we "prepared" for this predicted change in our market. This chapter will serve as a lens to focus on the issues that managed care has brought to the training of professional psychologists.

As I describe the changes that we can expect to take place in the training of professional psychologists, please remember that the part of "Chicken Little" has been played by those who have come before. The sky has fallen in ways that are more apparent every day. The challenge is for the profession to come up with a unified response that ensures the survival of the discipline as well as the continued care of those who so dearly need our service. My hope is that this chapter, along with the coping strategies offered in Chapter Five, will help those involved in psychology training programs to become better prepared for this rapidly changing world.

Accreditation of Training Programs in Psychology

Accreditation has served as the primary mode through which graduate training in psychology has been regulated in order to produce a somewhat unified product of relatively equal quality across different training settings. For almost fifty years, the American Psychological Association (APA) has served as the primary accreditation body for graduate education in professional psychology.

The APA was originally charged with developing a system of accreditation by the VA and the Public Health Service (PHS) following World War II, when the need for mental health providers in the public sector was critical.[2] The scope of accreditation has often caused contention, because some have called for accreditation to be separately defined for scientific and practice-oriented specialties.[3] Accreditation has survived primarily as a certification of the practice-oriented psychology specialties of clinical, counseling, and school psychology with a relatively recent addition of professional-scientific psychology.

The APA's guidance of psychology graduate study can probably be seen as having an extremely positive influence on the profession of psychology. The number of psychology undergraduate majors stands at an all-time high, second only to business majors.[4] The number of doctoral-level programs and students within those programs also is at record levels.[5] Postdoctoral graduate training is becoming even more popular as doctoral students seek further specialized training, and the APA Committee on Accreditation recently developed draft accreditation guidelines for postdoctoral programs.[6]

As the primary accrediting body of the profession, the APA protects the direct consumers of graduate training (students) by ensuring the quality of the product (education) they are purchasing. It also assures indirect consumers (patients, clients, and communities) that their providers have been appropriately trained in programs that have met the minimum standards of the profession.

APA accreditation appears to have become the standard by which those trained in professional psychology can be judged. Accreditation by the APA has been chosen by many state legislatures through their licensing statutes as the standard by which licensee applicants are judged appropriate to sit for license examinations. Likewise, applicants must be graduates of APA-approved graduate programs and internships in order to be considered for any positions within systems that employ large numbers of psychologists such as the VA. Recently, some managed care organizations (MCOs) have determined that graduation from an APA-approved graduate program and internship may serve as their minimum qualifications for participation in their provider panels.

Revising Accreditation Standards

The success of the APA accreditation process, along with its apparent endorsement by entities in both the public and private sector, might lead one to believe that the current accreditation process may be sufficient to carry psychology another fifty years. The problem, however, is that this process was originally designed for a system that had few, if any, third-party payers, and the original goal was to provide consistently high-quality applicants to internships at VA medical centers and PHS training grants. While serving its original purpose (and many others) well over the years, accreditation standards have been adapted recently to accommodate the rapid changes taking place in the current healthcare environment.

Over the past few years, the Committee on Accreditation of the APA has been revising the accreditation criteria for graduate programs and psychology internships.[7] The revised criteria that went into effect on January 1, 1996, clearly represent several major changes that may help training programs as they try to adapt to managed care. The new criteria require training programs to clearly state their model and philosophy of training along with attendant goals and objectives. Measurement of outcomes of the educational process is also expected. Although they do not explicitly state which models of training are acceptable, the guidelines do state that emphasis must be placed on teaching scientifically validated treatments. Finally, there appears to be a new expectation that trainees be provided with a curriculum that prepares them for the opportunities that are available in the professional marketplace.

Managed Care and Revised Accreditation Criteria

Although it would be unwieldy to describe the entire revised accreditation criteria here, I will focus on the changes that relate more to managed care. Some of these changes are clearly positive in their potential to better prepare students for the managed care market, but some may also make it more difficult for programs to function in that same environment.

Broadened Training Models

The new accreditation standards allow graduate and internship programs to choose their own models and philosophies of training, rather than being strictly limited to specific guidelines for curriculum. These models of training will be decided at the local training program level, but are limited in that interventions taught must be empirically verified (or verifiable if the treatments are new and innovative).

With managed care's emphasis on limiting treatments to only those that have become standards of practice, this requirement increases the likelihood that the programs will be preparing their students for managed care practice. However, it is quite likely that the treatments taught may still be considered too costly (e.g. exposure treatment of acrophobia), or too lengthy (long-term psychodynamic psychotherapy).

Focus on Educational Outcomes

A positive change relative to managed care will be the requirement to focus on measuring outcomes of training experiences. This focus parallels managed care's emphasis on verifying the outcomes of psychotherapy. In the former case, training programs are to develop goals and objectives for their students and then indicate what measures will be used to assess the performance of those students relative to those outcomes. In the latter case, students are more likely to become familiar with measuring outcomes in single-subject designs when they can use their own education as an example.

Effects of the New Criteria

The time that programs will need to spend to try to comply with the new standards will clearly be more than what was required in the prior versions of the accreditation criteria. The apparent trade-off is greater flexibility of program design for increased program accountability. Although graduate programs with faculty who are primarily pursuing academic goals may not be affected by this problem, internships and postdoctoral training programs probably will find the increased accountability too cumbersome to manage in an environment where survival is based on how well one can increase one's own efficiency. Recently, for example, I have had to increase my work week by several hours, am collecting up to 40 percent less per hour in reimbursement for psychotherapy, and face increased documentation and site visit requirements from managed care companies. Can we do more?

Accreditation alone, unfortunately, will probably fall short of the requirements of managed care companies for certification of training because there will be no standardized outcomes with which to compare students: both types of skills and competencies that are measured can vary significantly from one program to the next. In this case, the impetus to allow for more diversity of training experiences may inadvertently negatively influence the marketability of doctoral degrees from all programs. Of course, the alternative, to rigidly define program models and training requirements, would probably be met with significant resistance from many training programs as well.

Market Forces and Graduate Psychology Training

Unlike other business markets, the healthcare field historically enjoyed relatively little influence from the economic pressures of supply and demand. In the past, healthcare providers could set their own fees and increase those fees at their own discretion. As might be expected in an unrestrained demand market, the cost of healthcare rose precipitously. Managed care companies have attempted to restrain the healthcare market by placing restrictions on the diagnoses that can be treated, the fees that may be collected for those treatments, the number of sessions that will be reimbursed, and the providers that will be allowed to provide the treatment. The belief guiding managed care companies is that by limiting their provider panels to providers who are able to provide more efficient cost-effective treatments, they will ultimately save money.

While the number of APA-approved training programs in psychology increased by 54 percent in the 1980s, similar trends were taking place in the utilization of mental health services, and the cost of providing psychological care skyrocketed.[8] Most of the increased cost of psychological services could probably be attributed to increased utilization, which would not have been possible had fewer providers been trained. With increasing pressure to reduce costs in the provision of mental health care, the expectation is that fewer career positions will be available for newly trained doctoral-level psychologists.[9] Those positions that are available may be expected to have salary structures with narrower ranges than we saw in the past. Also, the types and kinds of training that will lead to success in a managed healthcare environment are likely to be vastly different from those that were available when few external constraints were imposed.[10]

Who Can Be a Managed Care Provider?

Control of the provider panel is critical to the managed care company's success. Managed care companies will choose who will be providers for their subscribers as well as how many providers will be on their panels. In times past, providers could set up a practice wherever they chose and associate that practice with whomever they chose, but now providers will increasingly be pressured to join large interdisciplinary groups that can provide the full spectrum of psychiatric care to their patients.

It would be unfair to describe managed care in generic terms, because different managed care companies have used various approaches to managing behavioral healthcare. These approaches extend from the seemingly arbitrary (session limits), to the creative (increasing copayments for extended treatment episodes), to the sublime ("just send us a treatment plan and we'll approve what you need"). For the purpose of this discussion, it will be necessary to classify managed care's purpose as providing mechanisms that confine the utilization of psychological services to those most in need at their times of greatest need. As such, managed care companies do best to provide their patients with the highest quality, most efficient, and universally satisfactory care possible.

Provider panels ideally will have only the best trained and most highly efficient therapists available. The challenge for managed care companies is determining who those providers might be. Unfortunately, there are no nationally recognized certifications for individuals in the provision of brief therapy, nor are there certifications, outside of the American Board of Professional Psychology (ABPP) diplomate status, that identify individuals who have excelled in their profession. There are few ABPP diplomates, and no other specialty certification that is recognized by the APA is currently available, so managed care companies must choose from available credentials that are held by a sufficient number of providers to fill their panels. These credentials include master's degrees in psychology, social work, and nursing. Providers with these credentials can usually offer their services at a more competitive rate than doctorate-level psychologists. The most readily verified credentials are licensure and program accreditation status.

Unlike our counterparts in psychiatry, who obtain their medical licenses while they are still in their training programs, psychology licensure is reserved for those who have completed their doctoral degree and usually obtained a minimum level of postdoctoral supervised experience. No comparable certification of knowledge and expertise prior to completion of the doctoral degree and licensure exists for those in psychology training programs. Thus, with no evidence available to show that psychology graduate students have completed a certain amount of required course work, or developed basic proficiencies, the managed care companies have little data on which to base a judgment of their credentials. Furthermore, as long as there is a large enough pool of providers who have those minimum credentials, it is unlikely that managed care companies will be sympathetic to the needs of training programs.

Where Is the Money?

A cardinal feature of managed care is the emphasis on reducing or limiting the cost of providing care to subscribers. Increasing the efficiency of providing that care is one strategy to reach that end. Other strategies include reducing the fee structures and limiting the number of available sessions that will be reimbursed to the providers.

At our facility, we have seen our fee structure for doctorate-level psychologists reduced by 16 to 40 percent over the past three years. We once had to pay little attention to the revenue generated by our interns, but we now have to consider how we will be reimbursed for every clinical care episode. In the past, the training of interns was subsidized by third-party payers through the direct payment of fees for services provided by interns or through the indirect funneling of excess revenue to training programs. Excess revenue no longer exists in a managed care environment. In fact, many hospitals, in response to the constraints of managed care, find themselves having to lay off staff, restrain salary structures, and increase workload demands to accommodate these reduced fees.

The economic constraints placed on the large healthcare systems that have supported psychology training in the past are likely to hinder or eliminate the possibilities for maintaining those training programs in the future. We have reached a point in the evolution of healthcare at which a crisis in the availability of training sites is about to happen.

The Market for Future Graduates

I used to eagerly hand over my APA *Monitor* to psychology interns as soon as it arrived so they could pore over the possibilities for their first postdoctoral positions. Many positions were also found through advertisements in local newspapers, national announcements of postdoctoral training opportunities, and the ever-present network of professional contacts. We also needed to inform our interns of when they should start searching in earnest for those positions, because they often needed these reminders. We educated them on what they could expect during their interview, appropriate salary levels, and how to weigh the relative pros and cons of their different career possibilities.

Today the task of guiding our interns to that first postdoctoral position is much more direct, though more challenging. First of all, our interns usually come to us first to talk about job hunting: their anxiety levels related to finding a good position have clearly increased. As they have already heard from their senior classmates, the job market is becoming more challenging. Second, they are choosing among fewer opportunities. Nonlicensed providers must find positions that will provide them with adequate supervision to achieve licensure. However, facilities are now less likely to hire anyone who is not already licensed because the license to practice is an easily verified credential that ensures a minimal level of competency. Opportunities in traditional fee-for-service agencies are therefore often limited. Even such healthcare behemoths as the VA are being forced to compete with managed care plans for the patient dollar, so they can be expected to respond in like fashion to these contingencies.

Competencies and Compensation

The kinds of skills that are required by employers are changing. Psychological assessment, especially personality testing, is being relegated to the "only when crucially needed" category as managed care programs limit the number of hours for assessment and treatment. It is hard to justify using up one-quarter of a patient's twenty possible treatment sessions in psychological assessment.

Employers are becoming more interested in whether their applicants have received training in brief treatment modalities and outcomes measurement. Long-term treatments are less frequently approved and reserved only for those patients with more significant impairments, so training in long-term therapy will be less valued. Broad generalist training is seen as an asset by managed care companies who prefer providers who have demonstrated expertise and training across several different specialty areas. Students from programs that promote only one treatment modality or do not provide exposure to treatments for large varieties of patient groups will be seen as less favorable.

Salaries, at best, can be expected to hold steady, but salaries may decline over time, especially for trainees and new graduates. The market for psychologists may soon be oversupplied as the number of graduate students continues to increase while the number of psychology internship positions decreases. More than 200 intern applicants from APA-approved programs did not match for internship sites on selection day in 1995 and more than 400 did not match in 1996. Competition from master's-degree-level providers for positions within agencies, health maintenance organizations, and private hospitals threatens to further dilute the earning power of new graduates.

Market for Graduate Professional Psychology Training

Although psychology has experienced a boom in the number of undergraduate majors (50 percent in a five-year period) and the number of doctorates awarded increased 41 percent between 1980 and 1990, much of this growth has occurred in response to the boom in mental health services in the 1980s.[11] However, shrinking healthcare dollars and the impact of managed care are quite likely to reduce demand for graduate training in psychology as potential students realize that the luster has dulled on this profession. Initially, enrollments will be down at the less prestigious schools, and eventually some schools may close. The recent difficulty finding enough accredited internship sites for qualified applicants is probably just the tip of the iceberg. As all facilities face increasing pressure to provide cost-effective care, practicum placements outside of graduate programs will dwindle as those facilities will see the activity of supervising practicum students as providing little benefit to the facilities (they will not be reimbursed by the graduate program or a third-party payer) at a time when productivity and cost savings will be the primary focus. University psychology clinics and counseling centers may serve as primary and sometimes exclusive practicum sites from this point forward.

Prescription Privileges?

The downsizing of the demand for doctoral-level psychological services along with the increased use of master's-level providers by MCOs appears to have spawned an effort within the APA to promote the training of psychologists in the prescribing of psychotropic medications.[12] This contentious issue within the psychology profession as well as between psychology and psychiatry could create a whole new set of problems and possibilities for psychology. Discussions of prescription privileges for psychologists have occurred since the late 1980s but curiously did not gain great popularity until managed care threatened the role of doctoral-level psychologists as psychotherapists during the past four or five years.[13]

A recent debate published in the *American Psychologist* has helped to highlight some of the broader issues surrounding the prescription privilege debate. Although it is not appropriate to describe the extensive issues in the prescription privileges debate here, I will briefly mention a few and then discuss the training issues in more detail.

Are prescription privileges a natural growth of the profession? Had managed care not come about, it is questionable whether psychology would have pushed significantly for these privileges. Therefore, many have seen the fight for prescription privileges as purely economic, ensuring the survival of the profession as its identity as the cost-effective provider of psychotherapy is eroded by equally effective care from master's-level providers.[14] Others have seen this development as a natural outgrowth of psychology's broadening perspective of mental illness and a way in which it could provide more comprehensive care to those that are served.[15] Others have mentioned the shortage of well-trained prescribers in rural areas and needs that are not being met by the nation's psychiatrists.[16]

The training issues have taken a backseat to many of these concerns. Psychiatry's stance has been that psychologists should not be trained because they could not be taught to responsibly prescribe in the time periods that have been proposed (anywhere from nine credit hours to two full years of supplementary training). However, issues of training curriculum aside, doctoral-level psychologists represent a group of extremely capable individuals who have already achieved excellence in their discipline. Clearly, they can be taught, as physician's assistants and nurse practitioners have been, to prescribe, at minimum, on a limited basis.[17] With the "can they be trained?" issue aside, the question moves to whether this is an appropriate direction for the profession of psychology. Humphreys dealt with this issue in an article on the history and future of psychotherapy in clinical psychology.[18] His historical overview is enlightening as he reminds the profession that prior to World War II, psychotherapy was practiced by only a few psychologists and it fell under the domain of psychiatry. Psychotherapy was adopted by the profession in larger numbers to meet the needs of returning World War II veterans, but this was initially done under the supervision and direction of psychiatrists. Humphreys adds that it would make more sense for clinical psychologists to look toward their unique strengths and develop identities as human behavior experts whose services are useful across a wider spectrum than just psychotherapy. Specifically, he suggests that psychologists consider working on social ills in the schools, in the community, and other arenas where their science can be appreciated.

It is too early to tell where the debate on prescription privileges will take the field of psychology, but it is becoming clearer that psychology training will have to change to accommodate reduced demand for psychotherapy among doctoral-level psychologists, and perhaps prescription privilege training or other new fields of endeavor. In the next section, I will describe what I believe to be the major challenges facing those who educate professional psychologists.

What Can Doctoral-Level Psychologists Offer to Managed Care?

It may be quite helpful for psychologists to examine the skills that are unique to their level of training. Historically, much of the research in psychotherapy has emanated from doctoral-level psychologists and programs. The demand for research regarding cost-effective care will be significantly increased in a managed healthcare environment. Psychologists may be able to provide that research and obtain funding from managed care companies for that research. Doctoral programs that de-emphasize research in favor of clinical training may find that their students are unprepared for the researcher role.

Doctoral-level psychologists are also more likely to have studied personality, psychopathology, and psychotherapy in greater depth than providers with less training. Though this increased knowledge does not directly translate into better treatment outcomes, doctoral-level psychologists may serve as supervisors to help master's-level providers in diagnosis and treatment planning with more difficult cases. Though managed care companies may not initially see this role as cost-effective, research will need to be completed to demonstrate the proposed effectiveness of providing "expert" supervision with difficult cases. Training in supervision, which is not part of the usual doctoral program, may be needed to fulfill this role.

Finally, doctoral-level psychologists are uniquely qualified in psychometric assessment. The assessment of personality, cognitive functioning, and neuropsychological functioning will probably always be the domain of doctoral-level psychologists because of their necessary training in test administration, test construction, reliability, and validity as well as their extensive training in test interpretation. The added value of psychological assessment needs to be demonstrated through research relating outcomes to the use of psychological assessment techniques. Training programs that have de-emphasized psychometric assessment training in favor of psychotherapy training will not be as desirable in the future.

—⚶—

Historically, the training of professional psychologists has been diverse in its methods and contents. The great variability in training requirements, along with the failure of the profession to carve out its own niche in the mental health marketplace, has led to a point at which professional psychology, lacking a unified training model, is being squeezed out of the middle of the mental healthcare continuum between psychiatry and master's-level providers. Ironically, the tolerance with which psychology has embraced divergent viewpoints in the past is likely to be a hindrance to professional psychology in the future. If professional psychologists hope to remain a major force in the healthcare market, they will have to work harder to clarify their mission, define their objectives, and set their goals to accommodate the changes brought about by managed care. Unfortunately, the market for trainees as customers of training programs is likely to be the most powerful influence for change in graduate training programs. Programs that anticipate that change now will probably survive and may well prosper as they work toward creative solutions to accommodate the changes brought about by managed care. Furthermore, it would be helpful for training programs to look into nontraditional clinical areas such as applications of behavioral technology to the work environment, government, and social programs to diversify the application of clinical skills. This diversification could insulate professional psychology against attacks that are devastating only because of the reliance of the profession on the provision of one primary service.

Notes

1. Cummings, N. A. (1986). The dismantling of our health system: Strategies for the survival of psychological practice. *American Psychologist, 41*, 426–431.
2. Sheridan, E., Matarzzo, J., & Nelson, P. (1995). Accreditation of psychology's graduate professional education and training programs: An historical perspective. *Professional Psychology: Research and Practice, 26* (4), 386–392.
3. Shapiro, A. E., & Wiggins, J. G. (1994). A Psy.D. degree for every practitioner: Truth in labeling. *American Psychologist, 49,* 207–210.
4. Murray, B. (1996). Psychology remains top college major. *The APA Monitor, 27* (2), 1.
5. Dial, T. H., Pion, G. M., Cooney, B., Kohout, J., Kaplan, K. O., Ginsberg, L., Merwin, E. I., Fox, J. C., Fginsverg, M., Staton, J., Clawson, T. W., Wildermuth, V. A., Blankertz, L., & Hughes, R. (1992). Training of mental health providers. In R. W. Manderscheid and M. A. Sonnenschein (Eds.), *Mental health, United States, 1992.* Washington, DC: U.S. Department of Health and Human Services, U.S. Government Printing Office.
6. American Psychological Association, Committee on Accreditation. (1995). *Guidelines and principles for accreditation of postdoctoral programs.* Washington, DC: American Psychological Association.
7. American Psychological Association, Committee on Accreditation. (1995). *Guidelines and principles for accreditation of programs in professional psychology.* Washington, DC: American Psychological Association.
8. *Mental health, United States, 1992.*
9. Belar, C. D. (1995). Collaboration in capitated care: Challenges for psychology. *Professional Psychology: Research and Practice, 26,* 139–146.
10. *American Psychologist, 41,* 426–431.

11. *The APA Monitor, 27* (2), 1; *Mental health, United States, 1992.*

12. De Leon, P. H., Fox, R. E., & Graham, S. R. (1991). Prescription privileges: Psychology's next frontier? *American Psychologist, 46,* 384–393.

13. *American Psychologist, 46,* 384–393.

14. Hayes, S. C., & Heiby, E. (1996). Psychology's drug problem: Do we need a fix, or should we just say no? *American Psychologist, 51,* 198–206.

15. Pachman, J. S. (1996). The dawn of a revolution in mental health. *American Psychologist, 51,* 213–215; DeLeon, P. H., & Wiggins, J. G. (1996). Prescription privileges for psychologists. *American Psychologist, 51,* 225–229.

16. DeLeon, P. (1993). Legislative issues. *The Independent Practitioner, 13,* 170–172.

17. *American Psychologist, 51,* 198–206.

18. Humphreys, K. (1996). Clinical psychologists as psychotherapists: History, future, and alternatives. *American Psychologist, 51,* 190–197.

Chapter Five

Creating New Models for Clinical Training in Psychology

Mark R. Lovell

As a clinical psychologist who began a professional career in the mid-1980s during the heyday of liberal reimbursement for behavioral health services, I have witnessed numerous changes in the healthcare delivery system. With the increased focus on the financial aspects of behavioral healthcare, I also have noticed a significant change in my own thinking regarding what constitutes "effective" treatment. More specifically, my thinking has shifted rather dramatically from conceptualizing behavioral healthcare in terms of effectiveness alone to a consideration of how to provide the best possible service while using the least amount of dwindling financial resources.

Since 1989, I have also had the unusual opportunity to develop a psychology training program that includes an internship training program accredited by the American Psychological Association (APA). I have tried to balance the rigorous training criteria established by the APA with the financial realities of having to ensure that the clinical productivity of our interns was high enough to offset the costs associated with the internship program. This challenge has been difficult for me as it has been for many of my colleagues around the country.

Psychology is now at its zenith as a profession and the number of individuals who are seeking graduate training in psychology appears to be on the rise. A recent popular magazine article ranked the profession of psychologist fourth of twenty-six professions with regard to likely available jobs in the year 2005, ranking only behind computer systems analyst, physical therapist, and operations analyst.[1]

However, while clinical psychology enjoys unparalleled popularity as a profession, several issues threaten the traditional model of how training is provided to aspiring psychologists. Managed care is having a definite impact on clinical training in the field of clinical psychology. In fact, over the last two years, the number of psychology practicum and internship sites that are available to trainees has not kept pace with the number of people who require training and hundreds of students have been left without training slots. Much of this problem is either directly or indirectly attributable to the implementation of efforts to control healthcare costs through the management of behavioral healthcare services.

Although this situation is making it difficult for many psychology trainees to finish their training, in the long run the field of clinical psychology probably will adjust to market pressures just as other mental health endeavors are adjusting—by evolving and adapting to better prepare psychologists to work more effectively within managed care environments. This task is a formidable one that will involve a great deal of coordinated effort by graduate programs, internship sites, and local, state, and national psychological organizations.

This chapter describes common questions concerning the viability of psychology training programs and outlines strategies for implementing the changes that will be necessary if graduate and postgraduate training is to survive in a behavioral healthcare environment that is increasingly becoming guided by managed care principles. The impact of managed care on behavioral healthcare varies depending on the geographical area of the country, type of institution, and particular penetration of managed care into the healthcare market in the particular state or city.

The current situation regarding managed care and training in psychology is dynamic and continuously evolving. There appear to be both short-term and more long-term implications for training in clinical psychology. To this point, short-term changes have been prompted by immediate financial concerns. It is hoped that long-term changes will result from more careful consideration of how to best serve the individuals who are in need of behavioral healthcare. Before detailing current challenges in the training of psychologists and detailing some possible solutions to these challenges, I will briefly review the current graduate training model in clinical psychology.

Current Graduate Training Model in Clinical Psychology

Most graduate training programs in psychology are based on the "scientist-practitioner," or Boulder model.[2] Accreditation criteria for graduate programs in clinical psychology and internship sites are based on this model as well. Although it is not the purpose of this chapter to provide a thorough discussion of the Boulder model, it is important to have a basic understanding of this model and its effect on training.

The Boulder model grew out of the rich history of behavioral research in experimental psychology in combination with increasing pressure for psychologists to provide clinical services in the 1940s and 1950s. This model emphasized the need for clinical psychologists to be trained in behavioral research in hopes that this ongoing interplay between research and clinical practice would yield advances in therapeutic techniques and strategies. In fact, this has been the case. Some of the most effective existing psychological treatments have been developed through the extension of findings gained through basic behavioral research to the clinical environment. Therapeutic approaches developed under the general headings of "behavior therapy" and "behavioral medicine" represent particularly good examples of the fruits of the scientist-practitioner model. However, notwithstanding the tremendous impact of the Boulder model on behavioral healthcare in general and the field of clinical psychology in particular, this model has been criticized on the basis that a training model that attempts to provide training in both the delivery of clinical service as well as in research cannot provide sufficient training in either of these disciplines. Perhaps the largest amount of criticism has come from more clinically oriented psychologists who think that valuable time during graduate school should be devoted to helping psychology trainees acquire more advanced clinical skills earlier during their training. This sentiment has no doubt been at least partially responsible for the recent proliferation of nontraditional professional degree programs in psychology (Psy.D.) and Ph.D. counseling psychology programs.

Psy.D. programs have stressed clinical skill development and have de-emphasized research skill development. These training programs have become increasingly popular among trainees who have their sights set clearly on a career of clinical service rather than on a combination of clinical work and teaching or research. Unfortunately, the sharp increase in the number of graduates of professional psychology programs has not been accompanied by a significant increase in the number of available internship slots nationally.

Counseling psychology programs have also come to represent alternative training models that are usually heavily clinically oriented, often to the exclusion of advanced training in research. Regardless of the type of program that provides clinical training in psychology (Ph.D. or Psy.D., clinical, counseling, or research), managed behavioral healthcare will prompt a consideration of basic long-term changes in the way that training is provided. However, several issues are having a more immediate effect on the provision of training to psychology trainees. The following section will address these related concerns.

Current Impediments to Certification

Managed care organizations (MCOs) in many states have been reluctant to accept psychology trainees as providers of behavioral health services to their enrollees. The impact of this reluctance has been felt most severely by internship programs. Although there are, no doubt, many reasons for the noncredentialing of psychology trainees, the primary reasons can be traced to

- A refusal to credential "nonlicensed" providers of services, including psychology interns
- The perception that psychology training programs are not financially viable
- An attempt to restrict the number of mental health professionals who are credentialed
- Concerns about the present and future ability to receive third-party reimbursement for services delivered by psychology trainees

Nonlicensure of Psychology Trainees

The model of internship training that traditionally has been endorsed by the APA requires the completion of the internship year *prior* to the award of the doctoral degree (Ph.D., Psy.D.). In most states, licensure to practice psychology occurs only after the completion of internship training *and* the acquisition of one year or more of additional postdoctoral supervision. This model of professional training is much more rigorous than the clinical training model in other mental healthcare professions and has generally resulted in a high quality of care for individuals requiring behavioral healthcare services. However, because of their nonlicensed status, psychology interns have been an easy target for MCOs, which are reluctant to grant credentials to unlicensed individuals because of concerns about the perceptions of potential customers. The disparity between psychologists and other behavioral health professionals with regard to licensure represents a catch-22 situation because the trainees need the internship training experience to finish their doctoral degree and become licensed, but they may have increasing difficulty finding an internship because of increased competition for internship positions.

Failure to grant credentials to psychology trainees suggests a basic misunderstanding of the educational process for psychologists because by the time they are ready for internship, all psychology trainees have completed several supervised clinical experiences. In fact, all APA-approved internship experiences require the intern to have completed a significant amount of clinical practicum training (usually 1,000 hours or more) *before* starting internship training. This level of practical experience, in combination with didactic coursework in required areas, ensures that the intern has had a great deal of relevant training by the time he or she reaches the internship placement site.

The unfortunate consequence of the refusal of managed care agencies to grant credentials to enroll psychology interns in their provider networks has been punishment of the field of psychology for having more rigorous licensure requirements than other non-M.D. mental health disciplines. The inability of behavioral healthcare agencies to use interns in treating their patients will, in the short run, result in the reconsideration of whether or not continued funding will be available for psychology internships. Behavioral healthcare institutions that serve mostly patients whose care is being managed will be reluctant to continue to fund internship training programs if they are unable to use trainees to provide clinical service.

A thorough discussion of the many reasons for the historical development of the current model of predoctoral internship training is beyond the scope of this chapter. However, the training model for psychologists in combination with managed care directives has at least temporarily resulted in a competitive disadvantage for psychology in the mental health field.

In the long run, organized psychology at the national level will likely make adjustments in graduate training program requirements. These adjustments will make it easier for managed care agencies to grant credentials to interns. In addition, as large healthcare systems begin to manage their own resources under capitated models, psychology interns are likely to become increasingly more attractive providers because of their relatively low cost. However, both at the level of the individual internship training program and at the national level, the field of psychology must do a better job of promoting the role of psychology trainees as well-trained providers of services.

Concerns About Cost-Effectiveness

Like all training programs in the behavioral healthcare field that flourished during the 1960s, 1970s, and 1980s when third-party reimbursement was readily available on a fee-for-service basis, many psychology training programs were not developed to be cost-effective and financially self-sustaining. Although the relatively low stipends (less than $20,000 per year including benefits) traditionally awarded to psychology interns have made the psychology trainee an attractive and low-cost provider of services in many agencies, some programs have more recently lost their appeal because of high indirect costs for maintaining the programs (e.g., compensation of participating faculty, faculty office space, and supplies). As behavioral health providers seek to decrease their financial "bottom line," some internship and postdoctoral training programs have suffered.

One particular concern has been the indirect cost of providing supervision and teaching services for the psychology trainee and the number of Ph.D.-level faculty needed to provide supervision. Some behavioral healthcare agencies are no longer willing or able to employ licensed psychologists primarily to administer training programs or provide supervision to unlicensed trainees. In training sites that are still in existence (outside of Veterans Administration [VA] training sites), supervising faculty are being asked to provide more direct clinical services that bring revenue into the agency. This trend is likely to continue, and training sites that want to remain financially viable will need to be creative in blending the service needs of the institution with the training needs of interns.

The issue of cost-effectiveness has been elevated to a high level of importance over the last several years and it will no doubt represent an even more important component of behavioral healthcare in the future. Psychology training programs will need to continue to provide training that considers the cost of providing therapy as well as attending to issues of effectiveness. Whereas psychotherapy research in the 1960s and 1970s concentrated exclusively on efficacy with relatively little attention being given to cost, current economic pressures appear to be forcing an evaluation of cost, perhaps without immediate regard for the quality of the service being provided or the long-term effectiveness of treatment.

It is also relatively easy to track and control the cost of providing the service but far more difficult to objectively measure the benefits of behavioral health services over time. A genuine understanding of the actual long-term benefits of psychotherapeutic treatments will take years and will be far more involved than the rather simplistic pretreatment-posttreatment ratings of improvement and customer satisfaction that currently constitute "outcome assessment." This situation is further complicated by the myriad of different treatment models that are currently in use in behavioral healthcare agencies and institutions. In addition, the relative merits of using treatments that may be effective in the short run but may result in eventual relapse in the long run will have to be balanced as these results become known.

Future efforts probably will have to devote equal attention to both cost and effectiveness issues. One interesting approach to evaluating these basic parameters of treatment has been used by Yates.[3] Yates has advocated an incorporation of economic cost-benefit analysis strategies into psychological treatment and assessment. This type of analysis goes beyond the traditional method of assessing only the short-term cost of providing the service and seeks to calculate what the long-term benefits are likely to be in dollars. The incorporation of this type of training into internship curricula might prepare the psychology trainee to work more effectively within a managed care environment and could lead to changes in the type of therapeutic training that is provided within a given institution. The use of cost-benefit analysis would also help to determine which treatment modalities are the most cost-effective and may help to guide the structuring of behavioral healthcare services in the future.

Restricting the Number of Providers

In considering the impact of managed care agencies on training in behavioral healthcare, it is important to understand that most MCOs represent for-profit entities that approach the issue of healthcare as a business and not as a philanthropic endeavor. Also, the more restrictive the MCO is with regard to granting credentials to professionals who are authorized to provide services and authorizing these individuals to provide services, the greater their profit. In other words, the fewer the services that are authorized and the less expensive the provider, the more profit the MCO makes. Furthermore, MCOs are largely unregulated at the state or federal level with regard to who they grant credentials to or the amount of reimbursement they authorize to providers.

Therefore, unfortunately, some managed care agencies may use the fact that psychology interns and postdoctoral fellows are not licensed to justify using master's-level providers who have relatively less training and who, at first glance, appear to be comparatively less expensive. Several legislative initiatives that may help to curb discriminatory practices by managed care providers will be described later in this chapter.

Concerns About Future Reimbursement for Trainees

Recent rulings by Medicare have called into question the financial viability of allowing students to provide behavioral health services. More specifically, Medicare has recently attempted to restrict reimbursement for behavioral health services only for the time when the licensed provider (faculty member or attending physician or psychologist) is directly providing the service. Medicare no longer appears to be willing to reimburse for services that are provided by trainees, even if these services are supervised by the licensed provider. This change in policy could have a profound effect on medical school and residency training and could reduce the number of hospitals that could afford to provide training to all behavioral healthcare trainees. With the recent inclusion of psychologists as independent providers of mental health services under Medicare, this restriction also could directly affect the ability of hospitals to use interns in the provision of services.

What Can Be Done?

If psychology training programs are to remain financially viable, administrative costs will have to be contained as much as possible. This cost containment will be a challenge given the current rigorous APA requirement that the equivalent of at least one-half of a faculty position be dedicated to administration of the internship program and an additional complement of full-time faculty to provide instruction and supervision. There is also likely to be initial resistance on the part of internship faculty who have typically attempted to separate training and clinical service needs. To remain financially viable, training programs will have to convince the funding source (e.g., hospital, mental health center, or university) that administration costs can be offset by revenues generated by trainees and by the overall enrichment of the institution by the training program.

Directors of internships and training programs will have to be increasingly mindful of the "bottom line" and therefore will need to structure training experiences so that interns see more patients than they might have in the past. This arrangement may result in decreased breadth of training for psychology trainees, who may find their training experiences increasingly defined by institutional needs as opposed to their personal training preferences. Ultimately, the need for trainees to render more clinical service will have to be balanced against the need for them to engage in other important components of the internship, such as didactic experiences and research.

Development of Consortium Training Programs

Historically, internship consortiums have represented a useful model of psychology internship training. In this model, the internship experience consists of participation at a collection of different training sites that are located within a specific geographical area. Although in some cases this type of training model could result in fragmented training, many of these programs have evolved into highly organized and well-respected internship sites (e.g., the Pittsburgh VA and Wichita VA internship consortiums).

Internship consortiums can provide a diverse menu of training experiences to interns at a relatively low cost to participating training sites. This diversity is typically not present in internships or postdoctoral fellowships that are offered within a specific hospital, mental health, or university setting. The training consortium also can spread administrative overhead costs over several sites. The inclusion of managed care agencies in internship consortiums would represent an excellent way for interns to receive training in a managed care setting. This type of training experience also would allow the managed care agency to discover the usefulness of having psychology trainees as providers of service.

Utilization of Innovative Supervision Models

Some psychology training programs, including our own, have effectively employed a group supervision model in which interns present case material and receive feedback on clinical issues from the supervising faculty member and from their peers. This model results in a higher degree of exposure to clinical case material than more traditional one-on-one supervision models. It also reduces administrative overhead by limiting the amount of time spent in providing supervision by internship faculty.

Although it would be unrealistic to think that group supervision could completely replace the one-on-one model that now predominates in the field (and is required for accreditation as well as application for licensure in most states), this type of supervision can serve as a useful adjunct to one-on-one supervision. In addition, it has been our experience that this type of peer-mediated educational experience can be a very constructive way of learning—both for the individual who is presenting the case material as well as for the other interns who can provide feedback to the presenter.

Inclusion of Voluntary Adjunct Supervising Faculty

The core of psychology training programs has traditionally consisted of full-time employees of the particular internship setting who are available to deal with any treatment issues that may emerge. However, many psychology training programs rely heavily on unpaid, adjunct supervisors who participate in the training program because of a commitment to the field or for their own professional enrichment.

Adjunct staff positions are typically attractive to psychologists in private practice because these positions provide the intellectual stimulation of contact with colleagues. In addition, most psychologists are trained as teachers as well as clinicians and enjoy the professional interaction with trainees. Adjunct positions also allow psychologists who work in private practice to become involved in attractive research projects.

Changes in Didactic Curriculum

In addition to dealing with the financial viability of psychology training programs in the managed behavioral care environment, the field of psychology must adjust the training model if psychology trainees are to be attractive to MCOs, both before and after they become licensed psychologists. Training programs must be redesigned to provide didactic training that increases the trainees' understanding of managed behavioral healthcare and provides specific training in the use of therapeutic modalities that are both cost-effective and efficacious. Unfortunately, this redesign is likely to be hampered somewhat at the level of graduate training because most training programs are located in university settings where they have been insulated from the effects of managed care. Therefore, there may be initial resistance to changing the educational model.

Training lectures and seminars should include exposure to administrative aspects (e.g., how reimbursement decisions are made, how to construct treatment plans) and fundamentals of utilization review. Ethical issues that arise in the managed care environment should be addressed because of the increased potential for violations of the patient's rights to confidentiality. The level of utilization review that is common in managed care agencies involves more individuals and therefore a greater risk of violations of patient rights. Ethical issues that concern the treatment of individuals who may have a limited number of behavioral health benefits also should be addressed. This issue is particularly important, because most managed care agencies impose limitations on both inpatient and outpatient benefits that can affect what treatment modalities are selected and how treatment is distributed or "rationed."

Training in Brief Psychological Treatments

In managed care settings, brief, symptom-focused treatment modalities are favored over psychodynamic or psychoanalytic therapies that tend to focus on more general issues regarding the individual's personality structure. The field of psychology has historically been responsible for the development of behavioral therapies in which response to treatment is empirically determined. In fact, psychology is the only behavioral science that is based on the application of scientifically determined principles of behavior to promote clinical change. Regardless of the potential usefulness of psychodynamic or psychoanalytic therapies with certain patients, financial constraints will likely lead to a decrease in the viability of training programs that take this approach to training. Therefore, psychology training programs must continue to include direct training in the use of brief treatment models and treatment models that readily lend themselves to the assessment of treatment outcome.

For some training programs that have traditionally provided training in brief therapies, this will not require much change. In particular, behaviorally oriented graduate programs that have always provided training in symptom-focused treatments such as biofeedback (for psychophysiological disorders), cognitive-behavior therapy (for anxiety disorders), and assertiveness training (for interpersonal difficulties) are likely to increase in popularity. Table 5.1 provides a partial listing of treatment models that are used in existing clinical, counseling, and Psy.D. programs and also provides information regarding the relative popularity of these training models.[4] Since the zenith of their popularity in the 1970s, behavioral and cognitive-behavioral therapies have continued to represent frequently used treatment approaches among psychologists. Behaviorally oriented therapies in particular have a distinct advantage over other therapies in that the goals are explicitly spelled out before the beginning of treatment and are outlined in terms of

Table 5.1. Percentage of Faculty Theoretical Orientations by Type of American Psychological Association–Accredited Clinical Doctoral Programs.

Theory	Mean (percent)
Psychodynamic	28.4
Systems/family systems	15.3
Humanistic/existential/phenomenological	11.2
Behavioral/applied behavior analysis	9.1
Cognitive/cognitive behavioral	49.1

Source: Mayne, Norcross, and Sayette, 1994.

measurable goals (e.g., changes in behavior) rather than less specific moods or feeling states. The goals of therapy can therefore be made explicit and therapeutic outcome can be directly measured.

Unlike almost all other models of therapy, clear goals make the determination of treatment outcome a much more objective process. The importance of the ability to document treatment outcome in a managed behavioral healthcare environment is extremely important. Although nondoctorally trained therapists may employ the techniques used in behaviorally oriented therapies, because of their formal training in basic behavioral research (i.e., learning and conditioning), psychology trainees are best trained in the application of these techniques and in the measurement of change that occurs as a result of therapy. This distinction will be important in the future because managed care agencies will probably become even more rigorous in their criteria for measuring the effectiveness of therapy.

Therapists who use nonbehavioral brief treatment strategies with therapeutic goals that are more subjective will need to document their effectiveness in meeting treatment goals if they are to continue to receive reimbursement from managed behavioral healthcare organizations.

Training in Brief Psychological Assessment

Just as the cost-effectiveness of different types of psychotherapy has come under scrutiny, the willingness of managed care agencies to reimburse psychologists for psychological assessment services has also come under intense review in many states. Whereas in the past many psychologists may have been called on to provide diagnostic information about patients through projective (e.g., Rorschach and thematic apperception) and objective (e.g., Minnesota Multiphasic Personality Inventory [MMPI]) testing, managed care agencies are becoming increasingly more restrictive about which services they will reimburse and the amount of time for which they will approve reimbursement. In the future, more objective procedures (e.g., the MMPI-2) that can be totally or partially automated to reduce professional staff time involvement probably will be more readily reimbursed, whereas projective measures that may require hours to score and interpret are likely to be less desirable, although there may be clinical reasons that these assessments need to be undertaken.

The design and use of computerized psychological tests that help to identify psychological disorders and lead to treatment recommendations will no doubt continue to be areas of growth. This focus on expediency is likely to have an eventual effect on the training of psychology interns and postdoctoral fellows because managed care agencies will be unlikely to provide reimbursement for lengthy psychological assessments. The supervising faculty member may thus be placed in the uncomfortable position of balancing the financial implications of allowing the intern to provide the lengthy, more expensive evaluation against the intern's need to learn how to administer and interpret the particular test. This is particularly true with regard to neuropsychological testing.

Neuropsychological test batteries that are used in many training sites have traditionally been lengthy and have been viewed by some managed care agencies as being overly expensive. In particular, the use of lengthy fixed neuropsychological test batteries that are administered to all patients, regardless of the presenting problem, have been popular in many settings. Although comprehensive neuropsychological evaluations are sometimes necessary when the results of testing are used to structure treatment plans, there are some problems (e.g., mild head injury, attention deficit disorder) for which the use of lengthy and expensive test batteries is likely to be viewed as being wasteful by managed care review agencies.

Many institutions that provide neuropsychological services have begun to use alternative models that emphasize a graduated screening in which more lengthy test batteries are reserved for only the most complex cases. This approach can represent a reasonable compromise, although neuropsychological assessment is dependent on a series of clinically based decisions that must be made by the clinician and this type of assessment model requires the most clinical skill to implement. This level of skill is likely to be difficult to acquire during the internship year and will require a great deal of supervision by internship faculty. Managed behavioral healthcare will probably affect postdoctoral training in neuropsychology because postdoctoral training in this area continues to be stressed as an important (if not necessary) component of specialty training in neuropsychology.

Training in Group Psychotherapy

Although most psychologists receive some training in group psychotherapy during graduate school, this has not been the preferred psychotherapeutic model. However, current economic pressures to provide behavioral health services at the lowest cost have forced a reconsideration of group psychotherapy as a potentially cost-effective medium of therapeutic change.

Training sites that wish to best prepare their students for the current behavioral healthcare environment will be required to structure training experiences that include advanced training in group psychotherapy. Our internship training program has found it particularly easy to involve interns in group experiences as cotherapists. This arrangement allows the supervising psychologist to directly supervise the intern "in action" while also providing an additional helpful therapist for the group.

Expanded Training in Partial Hospitalization Services

With increasing financial pressures to reduce the cost of delivering behavioral healthcare services, there has been a dramatic shift away from the use of inpatient hospital treatment services. This change has created the need for the development of partial hospitalization programs that deliver many of the intensive services that were part of traditional inpatient treatment models, but do not require 24-hour hospitalization.

The inclusion of psychology trainees in partial hospitalization programs represents an excellent way to expose the trainee to brief treatment modalities as well as group therapy experiences and also prepares psychologists for a possible role in administration of these programs once they finish their training. The use of psychology trainees in partial hospitalization programs also represents a cost-effective way of providing high-quality services.

Training in Preventative Behavioral Healthcare

Managed care networks are based on the premise that treatments that lower the risk of future disease or injury are preferable to treatments that do not address this risk. This is particularly true in large hospital systems that are responsible for managing the care of thousands of patients over the course of their lifetimes. Therefore, any procedure that can reduce the future use of expensive medical procedures or inpatient hospital stays is likely to be a good investment in the long run.

For example, a recent survey indicated that hypertension is the number one reason for visits to primary care physicians and the behavioral patterns that affect hypertension (e.g., obesity, noncompliance with dietary guidelines) are well known. However, preventative programs that address these risk factors are relatively rare and the types of treatments that go into reducing the risk of serious illness caused by hypertension are not routinely part of psychology internship training programs. Behaviorally trained psychologists can play a unique role in helping to better manage patients with hypertension (through weight loss programs and stress management programs); this area should represent a component of many more psychology training programs than it does currently.

Another example of psychological services that can help to reduce the risk of future serious illness or injury is to incorporate psychological interns into a program that we have developed to more effectively treat trauma patients. Individuals who are involved in an automobile accident in which alcohol is involved have a relatively high likelihood of being involved in a future automobile accident. Not only do these accidents often result in a tragic loss of human life, but these patients also use a disproportionate percentage of the healthcare dollar. Our program is structured to intervene within hours or days of the trauma to begin to address the patient's substance use problem and to arrange outpatient follow-up treatment. The assessment and treatment skills of psychology interns and postdoctoral fellows make them excellent participants in this type of preventative program.

Redefining Professional Roles

As mentioned at the beginning of the chapter, the profession of psychologist has become a very popular one over the last several decades with an increasing number of students seeking graduate training in clinical psychology. However, even under the most optimistic of scenarios for the future, managed care pressures are likely to result in a decrease in the number of jobs that have traditionally been performed by psychologists.

Despite this somewhat cautious outlook for the next several years, it is also very likely that, in the long run, psychologists will be increasingly asked to meet needs in the behavioral healthcare system that are not currently being met. As mentioned previously, efforts are being made at several internship training programs, including our own, to provide more broad-based training that will make psychologists more attractive as providers.

Although a shift away from doctoral-level providers to nondoctoral-level providers of psychotherapeutic services is certainly under way and is likely to continue, there also appears to be an emerging trend away from the use of psychiatrists, who represent the most expensive providers of mental health services. Managed care pressures to limit the role of psychiatrists to medication management will result in the continued need for psychologists who are actively involved in other aspects of the management of patient care.

Another factor that is likely to affect the need for psychologists in the future is the decreasing number of physicians who are selecting psychiatry as their specialty area of training. There has been a clear decline in the number of American medical school graduates who are seeking residency training in psychiatry over the last several years and this situation is predicted to become even more pronounced over the next decade. In fact, by the year 2010, there will be an estimated shortage of approximately 20,000 psychiatrists in the United States.[5] The void left by the shortage of psychiatrists is likely to be filled largely by psychologists working in concert with primary care physicians who will have to provide more psychiatric medication management in the future. If psychologists obtain prescription privileges, as is currently being proposed by some members of the profession, they are likely to play an even greater role in the behavioral healthcare system.[6]

This trend toward the use of nonphysician providers of psychiatric services has actually been occurring in some states for years and predates the introduction of managed care principles in many states. For example, one of the major factors that resulted in psychologists obtaining credentials as independent practitioners under Medicare was the relative shortage of psychiatrists in relatively less populated states such as West Virginia. In other words, it was thought that there were too few psychiatrists in states with large rural areas to adequately meet the mental health needs of the elderly. Although managed care pressures are likely to lead to a redistribution of some psychiatrists from major metropolitan areas to more rural settings, there will continue to be a shortage of well-trained professionals in many areas.

In addition to the ongoing redefinition of their role within the behavioral healthcare system, psychologists will be required to broaden their areas of expertise if they are to remain as an integral part of the healthcare system. In addition to their traditional role as behavioral researchers, an increasing number of psychologists are becoming involved in the administration of behavioral healthcare programs. Many internship training programs, including our own, are attempting to provide training in new clinical specialty areas such as partial hospitalization programs and consultation liaison services.

Despite the current well-justified concern about the effects of managed care on training in behavioral healthcare disciplines, one point seems abundantly clear. The need for behavioral healthcare services is not going to decrease in the foreseeable future. In fact, all signs point to an increased need for behavioral healthcare services as our society and world become increasingly complex and challenging. The challenge for all behavioral healthcare specialties, including psychology, will be to continue to attempt to provide high-quality care while being ever respectful of the expense that we create in doing so.

Notes

1. Wiggins, J. G. (1994). Would you want your child to be a psychologist? *American Psychologist, 49,* 485–492.
2. Raimy, V. C. (1950). *Training in clinical psychology.* New York: Prentice Hall.
3. Yates, B. T. (1994). Towards the incorporation of costs, cost-effectiveness analysis, and cost-benefit analysis into clinical research. *Journal of Consulting and Clinical Psychology, 62,* 729–736.
4. Mayne, T. J., Norcross, J. C., & Sayette, M. A. (1994). Admission requirements, acceptance rates, and financial assistance in clinical psychology programs: Diversity across the practice-research continuum. *American Psychologist, 49,* 806–811.
5. Pearson, L. J. (1992). 1991–1992 update: How each state stands on legislative issues affecting advanced nursing practice. *The Nurse Practitioner, 17,* 14–23.
6. Piotrowski, C. (1989). Prescription privileges: A time for some serious thought. *Psychotherapy Bulletin, 24,* 16–18.

Chapter Six

Current Training Issues in Social Work

Anthony M. Trachta

When I graduated from the University of Maryland School of Social Work and Community Planning in 1973, I was 23 years old and fully prepared for a career in clinical social work. That era in the history of social work was an expansive and exciting one. Coming off the initiatives of Lyndon Johnson's Great Society, social work programs had dollars to spend on the education of its practitioners, and schools of social work throughout the country were turning out thousands of graduates per year to work in this burgeoning field. I spent my two years at the University of Maryland among many students who did not have degrees in the helping profession at the bachelor's level. In the early 1970s, most graduate students came into social work as a default, rather than as a choice. The student body was made up largely of literature graduates and history graduates and students with bachelor's degrees in many other related liberal arts fields. Only a minority of the students, however, had bachelor's degrees in psychology, social services, or sociology. Even fewer, like me, had an undergraduate degree in social work.

My particular career path went as follows: three years working in two group home agencies for adolescents as a social worker for a residential treatment facility; five years as a social worker on a clinical research unit of a large department of psychiatry in a psychiatric hospital; three years as a supervisor, then director of a medical department of social work; ten and one-half years as a clinical services director and then vice president of a growing for-profit, privately held psychiatric services corporation; and now as a managed care director of the same large academic department of psychiatry. Very little in my social work education prepared me for this particular career path. The exceptions were systems theory, which I believe easily translates into corporate systems understanding, and social welfare policy, which, especially working in the public sector, prepares one for some management of the bureaucracy inherent in the public system and its lack of responsiveness to consumers.

Brief History of Social Work

The foundations of social work harken back to an era when large portions of the population were disenfranchised, poor, unhealthy, and otherwise superfluous. From its origins in the days of Dorothea Dix and her exposure of inequities in the state hospitals to its formulation as a profession in the days of Helen Harris Perman and the Foundry Movement to its current manifestation as the front line in the era of managed care, social work has always positioned itself to deal most prominently with those portions of the population forgotten and underserved by other professions. As the social cost of these populations was being realized in the 1800s, the individuals concerned with the welfare of the disenfranchised organized professionally to find ways of advocating for and allocating resources to these populations, be they in the state hospitals, poorhouses, or jails. These early idealists believed in the sanctity of human life and the sovereignty of human emotion. They also believed that with adequate resources allocated to them, improvements could occur, families could be held together, and the strengths of individuals and groups could be marshaled. This movement, which centered on work in the welfare continuum of the 1800s, stressed an overall systems approach that attempted to link charity, government, and public goodwill for the betterment of the lot of the disenfranchised. These individuals were not so much concerned with acquiring clinical skills as they were concerned with marshaling system resources for overall betterment.

As a result of their work, departments of government were created to deal with public welfare and public health, and charity efforts were directed toward concrete improvements in the areas of housing, hunger, poverty, and general healthcare. Although these government and foundation efforts enriched the lives of the disenfranchised, they also evolved into large departmental bureaucracies within most state, local, and national governments, and these bureaucracies created barriers to the delivery of care.

Still, it was becoming evident that their work was making a difference in extending the lives and general well-being of the disenfranchised. Social workers began to see that they had a place in the mental health continuum and that there was a direct connection between improved social resources and improved internal ego strength, functioning, and behavior. In schools of social work in the early to mid-1900s, this awareness translated into the development of specialized curricula that trained individuals in various forms of therapy. Those students entering social work education were encouraged to specialize as well as to receive a broad-brush overall policy education.

Nature of Social Work

Social workers tend to be collaborative and inclusive in their day-to-day work, and their problem-solving approach often works well in settings where intricate political and negotiation skills are necessary. In my 23 years in the field, I have observed many social workers rise to the top of their particular field either in clinical or governmental bureaucracy situations and evolve into true leaders. I have seen many more, however, either leave the field or get stuck in it, partly because of the limits of their education but also because of social work's position at the bottom of the hierarchy of human services professionals that includes psychiatrists, psychologists, and

nurses. Social workers have been at the bottom of the salary structure in those helping professions and have often augmented their
income by second jobs either in private practice or out of the profession entirely.

Even those social workers at the master's degree level who have
gone on to obtain their Ph.D.'s have often found themselves at the
"glass ceiling" of the professional ladder because of the limitations
inherent in doctoral-level endeavors in the fields of social work
education and research. Those with M.S.W. degrees who have pursued additional advanced degrees in hospital, health, or business
administration have fared somewhat better and in some ways are
ideally poised for positions in an era of managed care. This exposure to the various components of business understanding is necessary in preparing social work professionals for careers in this field in
the 1990s and beyond.

Six New Areas for Training

Managed care is a fait accompli. Anyone who doubts that this new
form of healthcare delivery will be dominant in the next ten years
is severely mistaken. Whether we like it or not, healthcare is
rapidly becoming a commodity with all of the various business
processes that go with it: consolidation, new efficiencies, reevalua-
tion, evolution, and applied business principles. However, a primary principle of managed care that eludes most practitioners is
that one cannot be satisfied with just assuming one's place in this
changing scenario and hoping that business will continue to flow
one's way. At some point either an agency or a group of individuals
will need to position itself at the control point of the dollars and by
doing so will have a large stake in the formation of any particular
delivery system. In other words, just becoming a member of a network doesn't ensure that one has a place in the managed care scenario of the future.

Players in this new market require new skills that are not taught
in the curricula of most schools of social work. There are six areas

that demand a better understanding by social workers for survival in managed care. They are

1. Legal and regulatory issues
2. Fiscal and reimbursement issues
3. Negotiation skills
4. Outcomes management
5. Focused treatment models
6. Case management

These new competencies can be acquired in a way that does not compromise the reasons one first enters the field. Social workers should be advocates for the people they serve. They should be intermediaries between individuals, groups, and larger systems, and they should be translators of the various languages one needs to speak to deliver healthcare in an ever-changing environment. Simultaneously, social workers who operate in an administrative capacity on a daily basis must preserve and defend their institution, position it in the new business atmosphere, and evaluate the outcomes of the services that they provide. They need to collaborate not only with other human services disciplines but with business entities as well.

The six aforementioned areas of focus for training in social work were gleaned from observations and discussions over the last several years from current practitioners in the field. These practitioners have managed systems both from an administrative and clinical point of view. These areas of focus apply in varying degrees to all levels and aspects of the field. I will examine them individually as they apply to the current managed care environment.

Legal and Regulatory Issues

When one thinks of managed care as it is evolving, the term "at-risk" immediately leaps to mind. Risk is used in varying degrees to describe the chance one takes in managing a population and its healthcare, but it also applies to the chance one takes as a clinician when one is faced with managing limited resources as markets move from a fee-for-service system to a capitated form of payment. For those operating in the clinical capacity, this is a daily concern.

It is, therefore, incumbent on social workers to have a more thorough understanding, not only of the various legal aspects of risk, but also the legal aspects of its consequences. This issue presents itself most often in the form of questions related to liability. As more social workers are in a position of telling consumers that their access to treatment is more finite than ever, they are often concerned about the liability position into which they place themselves. There are legal ramifications to issues of medical necessity, placement in level of care, and termination of treatment and confidentiality. Combine these ramifications with a new focus on regulatory questions, especially related to governmental sources of payment, program regulations, and legal requirements for reimbursement, and one can see the dilemma.

It is not unusual for a supervisory-level social worker in a clinical program in the 1990s to be required by his or her agency to reengineer an outmoded clinical approach into a new one practically overnight. The process of accomplishing this task goes far beyond retooling the clinical approach. It includes a more thorough understanding of the legal aspects of managed care contracts, regulatory requirements for the operation, and licensure of new programs. All of these aspects will affect reimbursements and outcomes. In addition, to level the playing field in all of these areas, social workers need to learn an entirely new vocabulary to be able to speak with legal and regulatory authorities and understand their concerns and concepts.

There are two ways to approach these issues to ensure competence. One is to add specific courses to the basic social work graduate curriculum that address new and evolving legal and regulatory issues for those currently in social work education. The second is to provide social work-related legal and regulatory continuing education for those already in the field so that a quick study at least gives social workers a passing acquaintance with this new and important aspect of their field. Both of those approaches require an investment of resources, but this investment is inherently worthwhile. The benefits will be demonstrated when a social worker can look at a capitation contract and understand both the liabilities and consequences inherent in it and when social workers are called on to interpret benefit plans and contracts for consumers.

Fiscal and Reimbursement Issues

The new delivery system of healthcare is based on theories of managed cost and resources. As the fee-for-service healthcare delivery system sails into the sunset, a new and thorough understanding of the ramifications of new reimbursement structures and fiscal approaches to the delivery of healthcare is important. Social workers commonly are called on to write a business plan or to participate in the writing of one when new services are being designed.

In an era of shrinking resources, no agency is going to commit itself to a new program that does not have a sound financial analysis to determine its ability to be at least "revenue neutral" for the first several years of its operation. If no attention is paid to training in the art and science of business plan design and reimbursement structure, social workers will be out of the loop when it comes to understanding what things really cost and how costs are met. Even those practitioners who choose to remain in private practice must have a better idea of what it means to set volume projections, cost per unit of service, and reimbursement per unit of service, as well as a broad, basic understanding of healthcare benefits with inclusion and exclusion criteria for various diagnoses. We must be aware of the costs of space, overhead, benefits, administrative time, support staff time, and information systems to be able to deliver a figure that makes sense in a business plan.

An additional issue that arises in the fiscal reimbursement realm is that of marketing. Once one has a more thorough understanding of the business principles that apply to the design and delivery of this new product, how does one bring this product to market, know who the customers are, and convince potential consumers that it has value? Heretofore, marketing has been an aspect of business not often understood or accepted by practitioners of healthcare. That is not true in this era. Social work practitioners need to understand and accept that marketing a new service can be as important as the design of the service itself. If one cannot convince potential consumers that the product has value, even excellent clinical programs will be unused.

Negotiation Skills

The principles of negotiation, though not labeled as such, are contained within much of the current and past curricula in schools of social work. As practitioners, social workers are taught that they can influence behavior, decisions, and the very thinking of consumers. Negotiation occurs in family therapy, supervision, and in basic clinical practice. Negotiation is often known by other names such as reframing, partialization, and conceptualization.

As it pertains to business, the ability to negotiate is critical in arriving at end products that are mutually beneficial to consumers, providers, and payers. This is especially true in the clinical sense, because social workers are called on daily to discuss clients' treatment plans with managed care reviewers. Typically, a concurrent treatment plan is presented to a reviewer, and certain resources are requested for a continued stay. The reviewer and the practitioner together arrive at the optimum use of these resources within their limitations. The art and science of this process is critical to treatment provision but often misunderstood by practitioners, who see reviewers as deniers of care, rather than as partners in the process. More specifically, practitioners and administrators in the field of social work must also negotiate pricing on a regular basis. Many benefits plans are not clear about what services they will pay for, and managed care companies are often unfamiliar with a certain type of program offered. Therefore, they are unsure how to pay for it.

Social workers must be able to understand and articulate the cost of providing this program inclusive of all the areas aforementioned and, therefore, be able to negotiate a payment rate that will cover those costs and benefit the client. Training should include this basic business skill and could be acquired by course work in basic accounting, finance, and human resource management. Negotiation also involves the ability to have fallback positions that can be readily substituted for aspects of care if they are denied for prices that are out of the range of payment. In dealing with reviewers, a practitioner should be able to say, "If you are denying payment for this level of service, may I offer something at a lower level of care that may substitute and still fit the clients' needs?"

Outcomes Management

One of my most frustrating experiences as a doctoral student at the University of Pittsburgh School of Social Work in the early 1980s was grappling with whether the end products of our programmatic efforts should expand or end. I can remember numerous debates with my colleagues and professors about programs and services that had been in existence for many years but had never been evaluated for their efficacy or efficiency. The belief by traditionalists was that once something is in operation it should remain so forever with ever-increasing levels of funding. This is no longer the approach. Every program must be able to evaluate itself or be evaluated by others. Managed care demands that outcomes be studied and reported program by program and client by client. Practitioners often are judged by report cards on their performance and responsiveness to consumer needs.

Outcomes research and evaluation are very complicated endeavors that are just becoming understood by specialists in the field. Social workers must participate in the evolution of outcomes studies in order to remain viable in this new, evolving delivery system. Participating in outcomes studies requires an almost uncanny ability to create "virtual" programming, that is, programming that is in a continual process of evolving that can adapt quickly to changes in clinical technology or reimbursement. This flexibility is especially important as reimbursement mechanisms for human services become blended and funding sources multiply. It also requires a more than passing understanding of how information systems can be helpful to this process. This understanding does not mean just a basic knowledge of computers and how they work but an understanding of the many reporting mechanisms that information systems can design and deliver, how to read those reports, interpret them, and accomplish a new program design based on the reported results.

Focused Treatment Models

Two clinical areas in particular that deserve review in this discussion of social work education are focused treatment models and case management. New treatment approaches and new models are exploding on the human services delivery scene. As social workers, we must allow ourselves to think "out of the box" about how to combine brief approaches with levels of intensity in ways they've never been combined before. As we evolve in our thinking from the traditional approaches to treatment (e.g., inpatient for acute illness, outpatient for subacute and maintenance therapies), we must include new concepts like intensive outpatient services (time-limited, milieu-based, intensive, acute services) to manage crisis and create hospital diversion. We should also look again at partial hospitalization not as a means of continually involving severely and persistently mentally ill patients in treatment, but as crisis intervention modes adjunctive to organized residential programs and housing management. We must reevaluate inpatient services and strive toward optimum use of this very expensive resource, including exploring the process of interdisciplinary treatment that goes on within the inpatient setting and the roles of other professionals such as psychiatrists, psychologists, psychiatric nurses, and rehabilitation specialists. We must continue to work together with these professionals to provide targeted programs to address pathology and we must collaborate with child welfare, juvenile justice, and social service endeavors more holistically. This is the right way to approach treatment and the way treatment will be paid for as funding streams collapse and resources diminish.

Case Management

Last but not least, social workers manage not only systems of care but the episodes of illness that bring consumers to these systems. The role of case management will be critical in the evolving healthcare delivery system of the next twenty years. Unfortunately, case management is a misunderstood concept that is often operationalized as the practitioner's control over the life and resources of a consumer or group of consumers. A new definition of case management goes beyond that very narrow approach and takes into account all of the resources available in a particular delivery situation and the targeted allocation of those resources for optimum outcome.

Case management uses all of the aforementioned new areas of understanding to accomplish new trends in practice and, I believe, transforms social work practitioners into treatment managers in the new managed care scenario. Case management in its modern sense includes management of medical care, rehabilitation, growth and development, social welfare, system enhancement, and boundary management. It requires a high level of organization, purpose, and consistency. High utilizers of both medical and behavioral healthcare require long-term intervention and management of their care to manage the high cost of their care.

Schools of social work should consider redesigning a degree called a master's in social work and business administration to train professionals not only in clinical systems approaches of old but in the business systems approaches of today. This degree would open the field to influence from other professions that are shaping healthcare delivery in the twenty-first century. Finance, law, and public policy could lend valuable information and skill sets to social work. One approach might include redesigning the field placement or internship component of the degree to expose professionals and students to business. Spending six months in a managed care organization (MCO), a healthcare administrative setting, or a healthcare consultant's office would open the eyes of many students who feel knowledge of administration and business is unnecessary or even inappropriate. It could also improve prospects for employment. Many clinicians have "crossed over" to managed care to become care managers in MCOs just as they have risen through the ranks to administrative positions in healthcare organizations.

—⚋—

The profession of social work holds promise for the future if there is a willingness to participate in shaping the values of insurance companies, legal entities, governmental departments, and research groups. These are the "at the table" settings where decisions are being made and debated. We should be preparing to take our seat. No other professional healthcare discipline combines these aspects of doing business in the managed care delivery system of tomorrow. Shouldn't social work, with its rich history of consistently evolving treatment of individuals and groups and matching needs with resources, take the lead in this endeavor?

Recommended Reading

Applebaum, P. S. (1993). Legal liability and managed care. *American Psychologist, 48* (3), 251–257.

Austin, M. J., Blum, S. R., & Murtaza, N. (1995). Local-state government relations and the development of public sector managed mental health care systems. *Administration and Policy in Mental Health, 22* (3), 203–215.

Becker, J., Trano, L., & Marshall, S. (1992). Legal issues in managed mental health. In J. L. Feldman & R. C. Fitzpatrick (Eds.),

Managed Mental Health Care: Administration and Clinical Issues (pp. 159–184). Washington, DC: American Psychiatric Press.

Dangerfield, D., & Betit, R. L. (1993). Managed mental health care in the public sector. In W. Goldman & S. Feldman (Eds.), *New Directions for Mental Health Services, 59* (3), 67–80.

Donovan, J. M., Steinberg, S., & Sabin, J. E. (1991). A mental health fellowship program in an HMO setting. *Hospital and Community Psychiatry, 42* (9), 952–953.

Drake, B. (1994). Relationship competencies in child welfare services. *Social Work, 39* (5), 595–602.

Feldman, J. L., & Fitzpatrick, R. C. (1992). *Managed mental health care: Administrative and clinical issues.* Washington, DC: American Psychiatric Press.

Fiene, J. I., & Taylor, P. A. (1991). Serving rural families of developmentally disabled children: A case management model. *Social Work, 36* (4), 323–327.

Lehman, A. F. (1987). Capitation payment and mental health care: A review of opportunities and risks. *Hospital and Community Psychiatry, 38* (1), 31–37.

Maguire, L. (Forthcoming.)*Advanced social work practice. A guide for public and private managed care settings.* Pacific Grove, CA: Brooks/Cole.

Mechanic, D., & Aiken, L. H. (1989). Capitation in mental health: Potentials and Cautions. In D. Mechanic & L. H. Aiken (Eds.), *Paying for services: Promises and pitfalls of capitation.* New Directions for Mental Health Services, *43.* San Francisco: Jossey-Bass, pp. 5–18.

Moore, S. T. (1990). A social work practice model of case management: The case management grid. *Social Work, 35* (5), 444–448.

Olsen, D. P., Rickles, J., & Travlik, K. (1995). A treatment-team model of managed mental health care. *Psychiatric Services, 46* (3), 252–256.

Pigott, H. E., & Broskowski, A. (1995). Outcomes analysis: Guiding beacon or bogus science? *Behavioral Health Management, 15* (5), 22–24.

Rothman, J. (1991). A model of case management: Toward empirically based practice. *Social Work, 36* (6), 520–528.

Simon, N. P. (1994). Ethics, psychodynamic treatment, and managed care. *Psychoanalysis and Psychotherapy, 11* (2), 119–128.

Strom, K., & Gingerich, W. J. (1993). Educating students for the new market realities. *Journal of Social Work Education, 29* (1), 78–87.

Strom-Gottfried, K. (1996). Managed care's implications for social work education. Paper presented at the 42nd annual program meeting of the Council on Social Work Education, Washington, DC, Feb. 15–18, pp. 1–21.

Wells, K. B. (1995). Cost containment and mental health outcomes: Experiences from U.S. Studies. *British Journal of Psychiatry Supplement, April* (27), 43–51.

Winegar, N. A. (1993). Managed mental health care: Implications for administration and management of community-based agencies. *Families in Society, 74* (3), 171–177.

Wolk, J. L., Sullivan, W. P., & Hartmann, D. J. (1994). The managerial nature of case management. *Social Work, 39* (2), 152–159.

Chapter Seven

Defining New Educational Needs for Clinical Nurse Specialists

Carole J. Taylor

While preparing to write this chapter, it occurred to me that since being appointed vice president for quality management in a small, privately owned behavioral healthcare organization four years ago, I have been on a learning odyssey. I remember attending one of my first executive meetings, where the details of a carve-out behavioral healthcare contract for a large managed care organization (MCO) were being discussed.

While I listened to my colleagues' comments, my respect for their knowledge of the how's and why's of this new managed care world grew, and I felt left in the dark. I was unprepared to interpret the melange of new terms like capitation, per member/per month (PM/PM), preferred provider organization (PPO), at risk, and covered lives. It seemed I needed an approved abbreviation list to understand the content of the meeting.

Through experiences like this one, it became exceedingly clear that however well prepared I was as a clinician and manager, through twenty-five years of experience in community mental health, outreach, university psychiatric settings, quality assurance, and private for-profit inpatient settings, nothing in my formal or informal past prepared me to function with the changing economics and politics of this new world of managed care.

This chapter defines the education and preparation that psychiatric mental health nurses must possess to practice within the changing environment that faces us today. It also provides a framework for dealing with the change that will face us tomorrow.

Historical View of Nursing

Nursing has historically been defined as both an art and a science. In 1943, Sister Olivia Gowan, who was a pioneer in our traditional education, viewed nursing as the promotion of the spiritual, mental, and physical health of the total patient. She stressed health education and health preservation, care for the individual's environment, and the provision of health services to the individual, the family, and the community.[1] Sister Gowan spoke as a harbinger for the role that nurses must assume in the managed care arena today, when care must be focused, planned, and managed. Because of cost constraints, the nurse may not be the provider of the total care, but now must be the facilitator for how this care is provided.

In the past, we had the luxury of ample time with patients to meet most of their identified needs. As a young psychiatric nurse during the 1970s, I worked with a great team of dedicated professionals in a neighborhood satellite office of a community mental health center. We were federally funded by the community mental health staffing grants that were then very generous and plentiful. We had the capacity and resources to meet any identified need ranging from psychiatric, social, and vocational, to housing and financial. If a patient needed food, it was easily arranged. If a patient needed transportation to a medical appointment, I would bring them to the office in my Volkswagen Beetle. If there was a psychiatric emergency, we would often arrive at the scene, without police intervention, to provide crisis stabilization or facilitate admission to the inpatient unit.

Psychiatric Nursing Today

In the variety of psychiatric settings that now exist, we can no longer be all things to all people. The care that nurses provide must be medically (psychiatrically) appropriate and we must be prepared with an overview of the total patient in order to refer him or her appropriately to other resources. Ideally, practice in an interdisciplinary treatment team consisting of a psychiatrist, a clinical nurse specialist (CNS), and a social worker is best suited to meet these needs—with support from the psychologist when necessary.

The managed care environment requires that all professionals be prepared with a scientific knowledge-based education. In addition, we must develop creative, innovative tools to design and build effective and efficient delivery systems to provide care. Using creativity to maneuver the system maze is necessary for patient management along a continuum. The CNS must develop both right-brain and left-brain processes, both a knowledge base and a flair for creativity to survive and thrive in the behavioral health environment.

Expanding Traditional Boundaries

Advanced practice nurses in the psychiatric mental healthcare arena must be prepared to function in expanded roles that may cross traditional boundaries and expectations. For the purpose of this chapter, advanced practice nurses are defined as those nurses who have a graduate degree and certification as a clinical specialist in the psychiatric mental health nursing field of practice.

Practice standards for psychiatric mental health nurses have involved treating patients in traditional settings: the inpatient psychiatric unit, chronic day treatment, outpatient, or in the medical unit with evaluation by a consult-liaison specialist. These settings continue to exist, but new settings such as intensive outpatient and acute partial have been added to meet the diverse spectrum of patients' needs within the boundaries that managed care imposes. In addition, the role and focus of treatment has changed in response to managed care.

In the past, the CNS role in psychiatric mental health nursing consisted of assessing, planning, intervening, and evaluating care based on a thorough review of the patient's psychiatric, psychological, physical, medical, social, cultural, family, recreational, and spiritual needs. Cost was clearly divorced from the professional's role, and the patient was treated until treatment was completed without regard to cost or length of treatment. Sometimes, the patient got better. If not, the revolving-door client was born.

Regulatory Shortcomings

Regulatory and licensing agencies have played a tremendous role in shaping this traditional framework, with an imposed bureaucracy of narrowly written standards and difficult to meet yet costly paperwork demands. A typical example is the inpatient psychiatric treatment plan that is mandated and scrutinized by every licensing, regulatory, and voluntary accreditation agency. The professional staff time, energy, and training that went into developing the perfect treatment plan were and continue to be costly and oppressive. Medicare regulations for freestanding psychiatric facilities continue to require that initial treatment plans be completed within three days and that a master treatment plan be completed in seven days with review every thirty days. These standards remain though an average length of stay in a local psychiatric unit now ranges from five to seven days.

The bureaucracy that monitors healthcare has not been able to stay abreast of the revolution now occurring. In fact, many state and federal regulations and standards have not been revised during my twenty-five years of practice. Consequently, practitioners are faced with changing our own practice standards. No longer can we practice without regard or concern for the cost of care or the outcome for the patient. "Ethical therapy must be, to some extent, cost-accountable therapy."[2]

Economic Realities: Then and Now

Throughout my formal education and professional experience, the economics of healthcare and the cost to the patient were rarely, if ever, mentioned. My only experience with healthcare cost occurred informally, during a clinical supervision session with a psychoanalyst in the early 1970s. Cost was mentioned as it pertained to the importance in the therapeutic relationship with the patient. The psychoanalyst believed the patient needed to be responsible for timely payment of bills for therapy and he taught us how to approach the patient. He said, "Patients will not value anything they perceive as free."

In nursing specifically, cost was a separate and distinct issue dealt with only through the financial department of the hospital. There were no "price tags" on supplies or medications. Nurses were required to list supplies used or stock medications administered (before the days of unit-dose medication), but never were they privy to the cost involved.

My first awareness of the cost of nursing procedures and care came to me through a television newsmagazine expose of hospital billing and charges. The cost billed to the patient for a well-known analgesic was, as I remember, approximately $7.00 per dose. I felt terribly guilty at that moment over the wasted sterile 4-$\times$ 4-inch gauze pads I used as a young nurse while changing a dressing; over the fact that I followed procedure in not taking the time to obtain a physician's order to allow the patient to use his own, already paid for prescription while he was in the hospital; and over the fact that I had not questioned the procedure at all.

Nurses were not taught to question costs. Supervisors, instructors, and mentors were interested in educating nurses in tasks, procedures, theory, and practice techniques. Patients rarely ever questioned nurses on the cost of their care.

Current Economics

Today, care is delivered with extreme attention to the bottom line. On entry to most healthcare systems, coverage is identified prior to or simultaneously with the initiation of treatment. That treatment must be delivered by a professional or facility directly linked to the managed care network. This change crosses all treatment boundaries and levels of care.

If, for example, a patient requires inpatient treatment, the MCO must first ascertain that the treatment is medically necessary. The presenting symptoms must meet utilization criteria and be serious enough to warrant an inpatient stay. An ongoing review of the patient's medical condition is conducted at predetermined intervals with the MCO. The treatment team, including the nurse, is acutely aware of the treatment care plan and what needs to be done for the patient to warrant continuing treatment. It is also critical to identify specific, attainable goals that can be reasonably achieved by the end of inpatient treatment through discharge planning.

The documentation of the progress of care must be integrated and demonstrate consistency with the treatment plan. The MCO generally requests a concurrent review of the medical record, but may also perform a retrospective medical record review.

New Skills for Nurses

This process, especially in an inpatient setting, places increased demands on the nursing staff. Many facilities are downsizing their full-time nursing equivalents. Acuity is higher than ever before, lengths of stay are short, and the number of admissions has generally increased. In several places, nursing positions are scarce. Nurses, if employed, are remaining in their current positions and are required to assume more responsibility with less support. Nurses who work in a variety of settings have told me that they believe care is compromised and quality is suffering.

However, the CNS, if prepared educationally to master the managed care environment, can make a significant contribution to fiscal accountability without compromising quality. For example, many CNSs are involved in assisting treatment teams with the development of clinical pathways. Clinical pathways are generally based on diagnosis or symptom presentation. This process identifies the care that can reasonably be delivered during an identified episode of treatment with quality as a prime component. From a fiscal view, clinical pathways demonstrate the product a MCO purchases from a facility or provider. Ideally, clinical pathways should encompass an episode of treatment through any level of care.

System restructuring, which is vital to survival in every healthcare setting, can also be best assumed by the CNS. Using a systems approach, he or she can provide the skills and knowledge to effect positive change in the delivery of care without compromising quality and cost.

Defining Practice Roles

In my new role within a managed care environment, I realized there were glaring holes in my graduate education as well as a dramatic change in my practice environment. The CNS in psychiatric mental health nursing is traditionally and formally prepared for several roles at the graduate level. These roles include clinician, educator, consultant, manager, and researcher. Although these roles are validated by the certification process of the American Nurses Association and are activated in a variety of patient care settings, they are not always easily or clearly defined. They often overlap but are never truly independent of the others. Combined, these roles are essential in the managed behavioral healthcare environment.

Table 7.1 describes what seems to be missing from the traditional graduate program for the CNS in a managed care environment. These topics are critical elements to be considered in formal educational settings. The five roles are outlined with learning needs identified from a self-oriented, consumer-oriented, and systems-oriented framework.

The CNS as Clinician

The CNS traditionally was prepared to function as a therapist who could provide individual, group, and family therapy in a variety of settings. In addition to these skills, nurses must now possess time

Table 7.1. Supplemental Learning Needs for the Clinical Nurse Specialist in a Managed Care Environment.

Role	Intrapersonal (Self-oriented)	Interpersonal (Consumer oriented)	Extrapersonal (Systems oriented)
Clinician	Time management skills Organizational skills	Theory Assessment Brief therapy Crisis intervention Crisis stabilization Treatment planning Case management Advocacy	Economics Credentialing Outcomes measurement Quality management Documentation Group practice Collaboration Contractor parameters Clinic practice guidelines Case management (individual) Adult learning theory Utilization management
Educator	Assertiveness	Diagnostic & Statistical Manual Subscriber plan Medications Developmental/learning theory	
Consultant	Creativity	Levels of care Consultation Group process Interpersonal skills Collaborative skills	Systems theory Organizational theory Economics NCQA Standards State regulations JCAHO Standards Total Quality Management teams
Manager	Flexibility Sense of humor Relaxation Risk taking	Marketing Management skills Public relations	Case management (aggregate) Economics Productivity Standards of practice Regulatory standards Ethics Focus groups
Researcher	Analytical abilities		Statistical methods Outcomes Health Plan Employer Data and Information Set (Hedis) Focus studies Trending/tracking

Note: NCQA = National Committee on Quality Assurance; JCAHO = Joint Commission for Accreditation of Healthcare Organizations.

management and organizational skills to meet increasing patient and paperwork demands. We no longer have the luxury of limitless time with the patient. Efficiency and effectiveness are key to delivery of care in a managed system.

Utilizing Brief Therapy

Clinically, brief therapy models must be learned to treat and prioritize targeted, presenting symptoms. Most patients have a limited number of outpatient sessions per year and may or may not have a copayment responsibility. In theory, this system works well with patients who are motivated and respond to therapy, medication, or a combination of the two.

However, a brief therapy model does not always address the needs of the patient who may have a serious and persistent mental illness. The challenge to treat these cases successfully within the present framework is fraught with clinical, fiscal, and ethical risks for behavioral healthcare providers and MCOs alike. The seriously and persistently mentally ill (SPMI) patient may become lost in the system if not aggressively managed, and he or she may risk loss of insurance benefits and treatment failure. The result may be tragic or even fatal for the patient. A CNS must play a central role in preventing these negative outcomes.

Managing the Acutely Ill

I have found that CNSs are poised to creatively address the needs of the SPMI population. Delivery of care in a natural environment, with the support of a team, is cost-efficient, provides a reality base for the patient, and gives these nurses the opportunity to intervene with family or peers. To do this, it is necessary be skilled at crisis intervention and crisis stabilization.

Acutely ill patients often have disturbing and frightening symptoms that may need to be treated more frequently, and nurses must have exemplary skills. Treatment planning must also be focused with a strong discharge plan.

Patients may or may not be initially evaluated by a psychiatrist. When necessary, they should be referred rapidly for a medication evaluation. We must give CNSs a strong background in pharmacotherapy in order for them to make appropriate referrals to the psychiatrist. Quick consultation with the psychiatrist when medication is indicated can shorten a treatment episode.

Acting as Case Manager

From a systems perspective, we must prepare nurses to provide case management, because the patient may move through a continuum of services during one episode of care (e.g., from an outpatient setting, to inpatient, to acute partial, with a return to outpatient care). A CNS can provide continuity and consultation to the direct-care teams who treat the patient at various steps along the treatment continuum.

To act appropriately as case managers, the CNS must be trained to understand the parameters of patients' insurance and to possess a basic understanding of healthcare economics. Nurses should also understand the credentialing process necessary to participate in provider networks, including the networks' educational, licensure, and practice requirements. As is customary in this age of accountability, the CNS must also be prepared to submit to a quality management review by peers, a review of medical record documentation, and an evaluation of the practice environment.

Nurses must develop an enhanced knowledge base of the documentation required in a managed care environment. This knowledge is not only in the interest of providing quality care to the patient, but necessary for compliance with the National Committee on Quality Assurance (NCQA) standards. NCQA is to MCOs what the Joint Commission for Accreditation of Healthcare Organizations (JCAHO) is to hospitals.

Outcomes measurement is also crucial for the CNS's role as case manager. It is no longer adequate to look at just the process, content, and task associated with the care provided. Nurses must also be trained to measure the successful outcome of care.

The CNS as Educator

In the past, graduate education prepared a CNS for the role of educator by providing a strong foundation in the domains of learning and adult learning theory. Nurses were prepared on a broad scale to develop teaching plans for both individuals and groups.

Today, health teaching and patient education still rest primarily in the domain of nursing. Now, however, a CNS must possess a sound working knowledge of learning theory, readiness for learning, diagnosis, treatment (including medication), creative interventions, systems theory, managed care, and outcomes. As educators, nurses must be able to translate for all consumers of the managed care product (including patients, employers, MCOs, and families) the content and parameters of treatment both on an individual basis and to groups at large.

The role of educator is a key, cross-functional one and often is difficult to delineate in its new form, because nursing has always provided health teaching. However, with adequate preparation, the CNS can educate staff, treatment teams, employers, potential contractors, and MCOs about behavioral health needs of patients with recommendations as to how to provide the care. This skill can be both a marketing and public relations asset in the managed care environment.

The CNS as Consultant

Traditionally, we have prepared CNSs to be versatile so they may cross many artificially imposed boundaries. This trait, coupled with a strong knowledge base in systems and organizational theory, often enables nurses to serve as consultants. This consulting may take place informally within the treatment team or formally in a titled position. For example, a CNS may be hired to provide clinical supervision to nurses at a generalist level (nurses with bachelor's degrees). Both the formal and informal consulting roles require that CNSs possess proficient collaborative skills, because this role frequently requires working with all levels of consumers within a managed care framework including provider groups, treatment teams, employers, employees, leadership teams, and other disciplines.

To be effective consultants, nurses need to have the knowledge and experience to effect change in systems; to view systems from a broad perspective; and to creatively develop new programs and retool old ones. In healthcare, the nurse consultant possesses the problem-solving ability and interpersonal skills to promote change at the direct-care level.

We must arm CNSs with a strong working knowledge of standards and regulations (NCQA, JCAHO, state, Medicare) so that they can translate these standards and regulations into the development of creative, cost-efficient, level-of-care programs (e.g., acute partial programs). CNS consultants also must have working knowledge of the healthcare budget and economics as they relate to quality-of-care issues. This knowledge allows them to be the "conscience" of many diverse teams to ensure quality behavioral healthcare for any and all patients in diverse systems.

A glaring void in present graduate education is the understanding of the relationship between politics and healthcare. Nurses could have a tremendous impact on national, state, and local healthcare policy development if they were formally prepared to consult in this arena.

The CNS as Manager

Graduate school taught me systems theory and organizational theory. My leadership and management skills were self-taught or learned through various continuing education conferences. To obtain skills as a manager at the graduate level at the time of my training, a degree in nursing administration was available. However, there were few definitive courses focusing on the role of manager. Clearly, on a graduate level, the clinical and fiscal/leadership roles were separate and distinct.

Today, CNS managers are vital components of all major treatment settings and must be well versed in regulatory standards, ethics, and above all, healthcare economics. CNSs must be prepared to develop business plans and a strong referral base. Provider contracts with MCOs also must be readily negotiated and interpreted. Equally important, the manager must be able to interpret quality care outcomes to consumers relative to the cost of service. A clear sense of public relations is also required, because a CNS will often deal with consumer complaints and grievances.

Nurses must learn to become leaders. Our employees are internal consumers who bring valuable skills and gifts to the organization. In turn, we owe them more than just a salary. The area of human resources management is extremely vital. Combined with the exceptional interpersonal and motivational skills of the manager, the new workforce in managed care can be an excellent, quality-oriented influence on healthcare.

The CNS as Researcher

The traditional research role for nurses has involved the advancement of nursing as a science by a commitment to investigate problems and concerns in the practice of nursing. Research is the method of generating new knowledge to further the science of the profession. There continues to be a great need for research in nursing. However, the managed care environment has demanded that behavioral healthcare consider other levels of query through quality management techniques.

As an advanced practice nurse, the CNS must be well versed in quality management. We must teach these nurses how to track and trend data and to develop focus studies. We must train them to develop the skills to analyze and interpret the data they collect and translate it into something meaningful for the system of care. The clinical decisions of nurses must be data driven. Measurement of outcomes of care in a systematized manner, a task that everyone in behavioral healthcare is currently trying to master, is critical to survival in managed care.

CNSs must be able to display data in simplified formats including flow charts and graphs. Learning to benchmark with our own data is crucial. Learning to benchmark in collaboration with other systems to determine if the data makes sense can provide an invaluable richness and texture to the data. The CNS has the research and statistical knowledge to conduct the studies necessary in a managed care environment, but nurses must learn enough about managed care systems to understand what needs to be accomplished.

Opportunities for Change

Educational institutions are attempting to address the dynamic healthcare environment, though the environment is changing faster than new curricula can be developed. Educational and healthcare institutions face a collaborative challenge to prepare and enhance the skills of the CNS. This collaboration must include a conceptual framework and a plan to address the rapid growth of behavioral healthcare within a managed care environment.

Marriage of Treatment and Education

The effect of managed care on psychiatric mental health nursing practice has been widespread. This deluge of new information and economic dictates coupled with new practice parameters and requirements often leave nurses and other clinicians confused, anxious, and angry. These feelings can easily be transferred to the patient, who is already vulnerable. If educational needs are not met, treatment cultures will stagnate and the quality of patient care will suffer. However, as shown in the following example, by making education an integral part of the treatment experience, innovations in patient care and improvements in patient satisfaction can result.

In a small, rural, freestanding psychiatric hospital where I was the director of nursing, we often treated patients who, among other problems, were survivors of childhood sexual abuse. They met criteria for inpatient hospitalization and presented with a multitude of symptoms. Primarily, they were often self-mutilating to the point of compromised safety. They often presented with symptoms of major depression and an imminent suicidal plan.

In an active treatment milieu, these patients were able to contract for safety within 48 to 120 hours and remain safe during their hospital stay. They were discharged quickly with a transition to a lower level of care, i.e., acute partial programming three to five days per week for a maximum of two weeks. These patients generally could transition safely back to outpatient care for continuity. They would sometimes have several short readmissions, but the continuity of care was available and designed to meet their needs.

We developed protocols or clinical pathways to treat this difficult group of patients within a managed care inpatient environment. Changes in the clinical pathway emerged over time, with input from both the treatment team and from the patients themselves. The key to the success of this kind of treatment milieu rests with the education provided to the treatment staff. In this case the staff consisted primarily of psychiatric nurses and mental health specialists who worked under the direction of the psychiatric nurse.

The treatment staff, as a team, developed the clinical pathway. The educational seminars that were designed and provided to the staff included

- Utilization management criteria
- A six-week series on survivors of childhood sexual abuse

- Self-injury management
- Safety contracts
- *Diagnostic & Statistical Manual* (fourth edition) criteria
- Dissociative disorders
- Multiple personality disorder
- Posttraumatic stress disorder
- Group work
- Art therapy techniques for survivors
- Documentation

In addition to this educational work, we held dinner focus groups with former patients who provided feedback about how we met or didn't meet their needs. These patients helped us to identify the strengths and weaknesses of the inpatient program. This rich experience, which helped us to modify our milieu, was a continuous improvement process with quality management oversight. It actively incorporated informal and formal feedback about patient satisfaction to promote quality change.

This project demonstrates that serious and persistent mental illness can be treated efficiently within a managed care environment. The primary resource allocation was initially very high. However, over time the return on this investment proved to be successful for both the patients and the hospital.

Bottom-Line Responsibility: Care of the Patient

Care of the patient in a managed care environment needs to be carefully coordinated and thoughtfully planned within a cost-containment framework. Quality care must be maintained and disruption of care minimized. This appears to be a simple process. However, the following case example demonstrates what can happen if attention to coordination and planning is viewed strictly from a narrow, cost-focused, user-unfriendly system.

An adolescent was referred by an MCO for a chemical dependency consultation. The consultant recommended inpatient rehabilitation. The patient had a prior history of an episode of treatment with a specialty chemical dependency treatment facility. The MCO denied the inpatient rehabilitation recommendation because of a lack of inpatient criteria, and referred the patient to a partial, day treatment drug and alcohol program with a parameter of two weeks. At the end of two weeks, the treatment team at the day treatment program once again recommended that the patient needed inpatient rehabilitation. The MCO referred the patient to a different, specialty treatment facility. This facility, unknown to the patient and inconvenient for the family, had a lower daily rate for inpatient care. The patient's mother vehemently objected for several reasons. First, the facility was too far away from home, and second, they didn't know her child. Once this concern was brought to the attention of the MCO, the patient was referred to the facility most familiar with the patient.

In the best possible world, this case would have been managed differently by a formally educated CNS case manager who was familiar with the patient and the patient's history. The outcome, cost, and patient satisfaction would have been different. The CNS would view the broader system and the risks involved with the disruption to continuity.

This example illustrates that continuity of care and broad oversight minimizes the risk of the patient falling through the cracks or receiving substandard care. In fact, in this case the outcome was extremely expensive. To manage in an environment that requires broad oversight with specific attention to detail is no easy task. It presents challenges and opportunities for change and growth. The CNS, if adequately prepared and armed with the necessary information, education, and tools, is in an exciting position to make a difference. At the CNS or advanced-practice level, this collaborative role surpasses the artificially imposed boundaries of, for example, an inpatient unit. This role can ensure that the patient is transitioned from one level of care to another and demonstrates accountability for outcomes of care involving the patient and the healthcare team.

Where Do We Go from Here?

Organized care delivery in a behavioral healthcare system includes assessment, planning, structured interventions, and evaluation of outcome with an emphasis on coordination. This is the nursing process in action. Nurses have been undersocialized into a system, though, where they lack power to develop healthcare delivery patterns and are often sheltered from the economic impact of their actions, because of their order in the delivery system. Being successful in this new practice environment requires different thinking. The nursing process must focus on outcomes rather than tasks and processes.[3] Nurses should view all tasks and processes and then challenge the effect on the outcome of care. However, nurses must be taught the critical thinking skills necessary to ask the questions.

Within managed care, consumer satisfaction is a critical element in the healthcare delivery system. Consumers are defined as customers, and there are many consumers of care: the patient, their families, the employer, the primary care provider, and the behavioral healthcare provider.

Nursing has always considered the patient to be the customer, but adequate care for patients now requires an expansion of the nurse's knowledge base. Consumers have always been given choices within the healthcare environment. Those choices still exist, but in a narrow, circumscribed network of providers. With the many choices available to consumers, a paradigm shift toward satisfaction may be the most critical factor in the success or failure of specific MCOs and their healthcare providers.

Nurse educators and educational institutions must begin to integrate healthcare economics into the core nursing curriculum rather than using business electives to complement the core curriculum. There must be a closer marriage between practice and education.

Recently, I attended a reception at a university to explore the doctoral program there. A professor of nursing asked what my area of research would be. When I replied that I would be interested in research related to managed behavioral healthcare, she stated, "No, it must be a clinical focus." My concern is that educators themselves may not understand the changing managed care environment that links care and cost.

Quality management needs to be a central educational requirement for advanced practice nurses because of the strong quality management focus throughout all of healthcare. It can be the thread that weaves patient care and cost together with positive results, ensuring the future growth and development of behavioral healthcare.

Notes

1. Gowan, S. M. O. (1944). Administration of college and university programs in nursing, from the viewpoint of nurse education. *Proceedings of the workshop on administration of college programs in nursing*. Washington, DC: Catholic University of American Press, p. 10.
2. Wylie, M. S. (1995, September/October). The new visionaries. *The Family Therapy Networker*, p. 35.
3. Harrigan, R. C. (1995). Health care reform: Impact of managed care on perinatal and neonatal care delivery and education. *Journal of Perinatal and Neonatal Nursing, 8* (4), 48.

Chapter Eight

A Managed Care Organization's View of Training and Research

Mark G. Fuller

As a medical director with a large managed care organization (MCO) in Pennsylvania, I spend a great deal of time each day talking with other mental health clinicians. These conversations involve utilization review decisions, administrative problems, or resolution of difficulties to do with various patient care issues (such as access to care). Some of these mental health professionals are thriving in the current environment, whereas others seem "hopeless and helpless" in the managed care era. Most professionals I speak with are bright, dedicated clinicians who have devoted their lives to the alleviation of suffering from mental illness. So why are some of them overseeing active growing practices, whereas others are spending increasing amounts of time on seemingly unimportant "administrative" items while watching their referrals dwindle? I believe that one of the biggest obstacles for most clinicians is their training. Although the clinical skills and experience we have gained during our student days form the bedrock of our professional expertise, other aspects of our training may serve as a detriment when it comes to working in today's managed care environment.

One of my earliest experiences in recognizing the dysfunctional aspects of our healthcare system came during a public health course in my second year of medical school. While exploring the various healthcare problems facing our society (nicotine addiction, lack of access to care, drug abuse, etc.), it became clear that many of these problems could not be addressed by our poorly organized healthcare delivery system. This system, which was composed of clinicians in solo or small group practices and reimbursed on a fee-for-service basis, provided little incentive to look beyond the well-being of those patients who appeared on our doorstep. In addition, our responsibility for these patients seldom extended beyond the time when they were sick. There was little motivation—or financial incentive—to intervene with people before they become ill and little contact with them after they recovered unless they developed a chronic condition.

As I completed my training and began a career as a practitioner, teacher, and researcher, I was well rewarded by our system for my success. I was able to help many people and I derived tremendous satisfaction from my work. However, I was also aware of the continuing "healthcare crisis" of rising costs and difficulty with access to care. I worked at an urban teaching hospital at the time, and I was extremely concerned about the difficulty many of the community's poorest patients had accessing appropriate healthcare. This hospital provided services to all members of the community regardless of the patient's ability to pay and it was gratifying to work there. Yet most of our services were confined to acute interventions after a person had become ill. There was no system, or incentive, to reach out into the community to develop the kind of prevention programs and access to ongoing primary care services that could make a real difference in the long-term health of the community. Our country was developing a two-tiered healthcare system for the "haves" (the insured) and the "have-nots" (the uninsured or the partially insured).

Personally, I have been very fortunate in this area. I have had access to good health insurance throughout my life. As a physician, I also have become a very sophisticated consumer of healthcare. This combination has resulted in excellent medical care for myself and my family. I did not have to look very far, however, to see many people for whom our healthcare system just doesn't work. People on medical assistance have become truly second-class citizens in many institutions. Even worse off are those who make too much money to receive medical assistance but cannot afford adequate health insurance (the working poor). For these friends, neighbors, mothers, fathers and—all too often— children, all the high-tech medical gadgetry in the world is useless because it is beyond their reach. Our healthcare system has truly failed these people. I realize that some believe healthcare is not a right but a consumable luxury that some can afford and some cannot. I vehemently disagree with that position and offer the rest of the industrialized world as proof that adequate access to healthcare for all is readily obtainable with the right system.

This growing unease with our current healthcare system prompted me to leave my clinical practice and join a managed care company. I was growing increasingly uncomfortable being a part of a system that was so fundamentally broken. The financial success and prestige that accompanied my practice brought little comfort to me when I saw how others were suffering. I initially took some comfort in the effort to reform healthcare that accompanied President Clinton's 1992 presidential campaign and subsequent election. It was extremely disappointing to me to see this important initiative disintegrate into a fight over narrow economic self-interest as a variety of special interests tried to advance their specific economic agendas at the expense of the greater good. Also, it was disheartening to see how many groups who are currently benefiting from the existing dysfunctional system worked to block any reform, even though millions of people may have benefitted. I decided I could no longer "sit on the sidelines." Now I believe that I was secretly rooting for a political solution to our healthcare crisis so that I wouldn't have to get directly involved. If the political system would handle it, then I could just continue to practice medicine and I wouldn't have to become personally involved in the difficult work of healthcare reform.

I Join an MCO

As I looked for an opportunity to make a difference in our system, I became increasingly aware that healthcare reform was going on anyway. It wasn't being done by the government, but by MCOs.

These companies were changing the healthcare landscape right under our feet. Admittedly, some of this change has occurred solely because of economic interests, but some of it has had significantly positive effects. For instance, the entire medical assistance population of Tennessee was recently moved to managed care plans.[1] The savings were so significant that healthcare coverage could be extended to many formerly uninsured "working poor" residents.

I joined a managed care company because of this kind of potential. I hope to be a part of a revolution in healthcare that increases access and quality while decreasing costs. If this revolution is led by men and women with dedication and heart, it will improve the quality of life for millions of Americans for generations to come. If it is done out of narrow economic self-interest only, I believe that a political solution will be imposed on us that may not meet our needs as individuals or as a society.

What's Wrong with Academia?

Many of us trained at academic institutions that are notorious for their inefficiency. As a medical student, I was often praised for going the extra mile in ordering some unusual diagnostic test in pursuit of a rare diagnosis. However, I cannot recall receiving even a single compliment for exercising restraint and declining to order a test or procedure that would not clearly contribute to a patient's well-being. In fact, just the opposite often occurred. If a medical student does not work up every last possibility (no matter how remote), he or she may be severely and publicly reprimanded for negligence. This reprimand is usually justified as part of the learning process. A common practice in teaching programs is to pursue some diagnoses as an "academic exercise." This phrase refers to a test or procedure that may impart some degree of learning to the student but usually provides little, if any, substantial benefit to the patient. However, these learning experiences have a powerful effect on the practice patterns of students after they complete their training and go into practice.

Structural Inefficiency

The makeup and functioning of an academic training center often discourage efficiency. Universities are designed to serve as places where clinicians can research disease processes and reflect on diagnostic dilemmas while teaching students. Until very recently, the financial incentives for academicians were unrelated to the efficient practice of medicine. With tenure, some senior clinicians had little motivation to develop cost-effective treatments.

Impact of Incentives

At one time I worked on a twenty-eight-day inpatient drug and alcohol treatment unit. It was a very effective program and was staffed by talented and dedicated personnel. However, when we began to admit more patients who had utilization review requirements, I began to notice the inefficiency of our model. Although our patients did well, I became increasingly aware of the research that demonstrated the efficacy of outpatient models for the treatment of substance abuse. As I reviewed cases with managed care companies, it was increasingly difficult to respond to all of their questions regarding my continued hospitalization of otherwise healthy and stable patients. In part because of these reviews, I approached our senior management about opening an outpatient program for the treatment of addiction. My suggestions fell on deaf ears and I was accused of heresy. They asked how could I have strayed so far from "the faith." They suggested that only inpatient treatment for addiction is the true path to recovery. When I began to cite the literature on the effectiveness of outpatient treatment, their eyes glazed over and the matter was dropped. I was perplexed by this response from otherwise intelligent and reasonable people. I concluded that just as our patients had become hooked on the "high" of alcohol and other drugs, our management had become "hooked" on the financial support that goes along with a full, bustling inpatient rehabilitation service. Inpatient units like ours could be jeopardized by the juxtaposition of less expensive outpatient programs. The hospital had no incentive, and thus no interest, in developing alternative services. In all fairness, the facility would have been "punished" for developing this alternative low-cost service by decreased reimbursement from third-party payers.

This anecdote highlights one of the fundamental problems of our old paradigm. That is, there exists no financial incentive or support for developing alternatives to costly intensive services. As our teaching centers reinforce this model, we as students adopt it in our own practice patterns, and in practice this model is reinforced by higher reimbursement.

The Current Environment

Academic training centers have provided our country with some of the finest clinicians in the world. Unfortunately, they have also perpetuated and institutionalized some significant liabilities for their trainees and for our healthcare system. The main problems appear to be in four areas:

1. Lack of attention to cost
2. Lack of attention to outcomes
3. Lack of attention to customer service
4. Lack of coordination of services

Lack of Attention to Cost

One of the most important gaps in training comes in the area of cost. An estimated 80 percent of all healthcare costs are under the control of the physician, yet very few clinicians have any idea of the cost of most healthcare services.[2] As a resident I participated in a study to demonstrate how alerting healthcare professionals to the costs of the services they ordered affected "test ordering behavior." As you might guess, use went down when clinicians became aware of the costs. Also, despite the results of this and other studies linking decreased use to awareness of cost, universities and other hospitals did not adopt policies to routinely inform clinicians of the effect of their decisions on the cost of healthcare. In light of the negative impact that this process might have on their financial stability, one can understand their reluctance to further publicize this information.

In some ways our healthcare system has become similar to a large department store where the shopper (i.e., the patient) never receives a bill. Under these circumstances, "shoppers" will not be price sensitive when making purchases and instead will rely on other things to guide their buying. Their "shopping guides" (i.e., healthcare professionals) may become their most important sources of information and advice in guiding their decisions. What happens if the shopping guide is not only insensitive to issues of pricing, but is actually unaware of the costs of the store's items? The store's vested interest in profiting by an increased use of services further leads to the kind of runaway costs and excessive use that characterize our current healthcare environment. This is not to portray all healthcare professionals and institutions as greedy and motivated only by narrow self-interest. The overwhelming majority of people I have worked with in healthcare are honest, compassionate, well-meaning people. Even good people, however, are sensitive to incentives, and when a particular behavior pattern is reinforced again and again, it gradually has a significant impact on the entire system. The incentives within our system have favored the delivery of more healthcare, not better health.

Lack of Attention to Outcomes

In the field of behavioral health, as well as other areas of the healthcare system, insufficient attention has been paid to the question of what works. Practice patterns and psychotherapeutic schools of thought have developed without rigorous scientific attention to what really improves health and what is merely a promising idea. Our lack of interest in this area has allowed several decidedly unproved techniques and points of view to present themselves as being equally efficacious as more mainstream approaches. Without firm scientific evidence to back up our therapeutic approaches, it becomes difficult for those outside of our field to differentiate those people in true behavioral healthcare from quacks. We run the risk of being tarred with the same brush as less scrupulous practitioners who are using unproved processes and making unrealistic claims about their effectiveness. Our academic centers have not always been rigorous in their demonstration of proved psychotherapeutic approaches, so some third-party payers have concluded that there is little difference among mental health providers. They thus choose to discriminate among them based on other factors (e.g., price, location, and marketing departments). If high-quality, scientifically proved behavioral health interventions are to become available to everyone, academic centers must do a better job of demonstrating and documenting the outcomes of these techniques instead of tolerating outdated or unproved schools of thought simply because a prestigious person within the university happens to believe that particular theory. Beliefs are interesting, but scientific evidence rules.

Lack of Attention to Customer Service

One of the areas where most training programs really do a disservice to trainees is in teaching them how to provide good service.[3]

Many academic institutions are designed primarily for the convenience of the hospital, the clinicians, or their research needs. Too many facilities have not taken the time and effort to discover how user-friendly or unfriendly they are and then make the appropriate adjustments. It is difficult and painstaking work to design healthcare systems that are easy for the patient to use, but these accessible systems will be key requirements for success in a managed care environment.

If you have received care at academic medical centers, you understand the lack of attention to issues of customer service. Bed baths at 5 a.m. and routine vital signs at 6 a.m. do not promote satisfied patients.

Lack of Coordination of Services

Another part of behavioral healthcare that has caused significant problems for patients is the lack of coordination of services. This problem is so widespread in healthcare that some writers balk at even using the term "system" to describe healthcare in our country.[4] A more appropriate description would be a group of stand-alone hospitals, clinics, academic centers, and community mental health centers, along with a dizzying variety of mental health clinicians in solo practice or any number of small and large group affiliations. Virtually none of these entities tries to interface smoothly and effectively with the others. Even within one institution there may be fierce rivalries (ideological and otherwise) and competition for scarce resources. This competition results in little cooperation among programs.

This disjointed arrangement is clear to patients who are in outpatient therapy and require hospitalization. Unless the mental health clinician is also doing inpatient work (and is on staff at the facility where the patient is hospitalized), there may be little continuity for the patient.

While working at an inpatient psychiatry unit at an academic medical center, I saw inpatient clinicians make significant changes in a patient's therapeutic treatment program (pharmacological as well as psychotherapeutic) without consulting the patient's therapist. Outpatient therapists often have a longer relationship with the patient and are responsible for carrying out the plan after discharge, so I was amazed at this lack of coordination. In response to this experience, I routinely consulted the outpatient clinician about hospitalized patients and was rewarded with a wealth of information regarding what has and what has not worked in the past. In addition, I also got a feel for what the outpatient clinician agreed with and was prepared to follow through with as well as what interventions would be a waste of my time. For their part, the outpatient clinicians routinely expressed their appreciation (and their surprise) at being included in the inpatient treatment planning process.

In summary, although they usually provide outstanding clinical training, teaching programs have not properly prepared their trainees for the current practice environment. They have often avoided issues of cost and coordination, and instead they have encouraged the perpetuation of inefficient and customer-insensitive practice patterns.

The Future

Academic training centers are responsible for most of what is great in the field of mental health today. Without their ongoing contribution to training and research we would not have the benefit of their continued clinical advances or the addition of new clinicians. However, I believe that the current state of affairs in the field of behavioral health could deteriorate into a cold war between insurers and providers. In this scenario, there would continue to be misaligned incentives and both sides would be engaged in a "win-lose" relationship. Providers would be angry and frustrated as they watch their autonomy and their incomes erode while insurers would see little real progress in improving quality and reducing costs. Every cost savings for the payer would be money out of the provider's pocket. With little incentive to become more efficient, providers would cling to their current practice patterns and do battle with the payers through national and state legislation and the court system. The real losers would be the patients who would be caught in the middle of a system that could not or would not serve their needs. Instead, our healthcare system would exist as a compromise between two warring camps who could not find a common ground.

Win-Win

This process could turn out quite differently. I believe that on a deep, fundamental level, we are all interested in the same thing: high-quality outcomes in a user-friendly system with reasonable costs. What insurer, provider, or patient could argue with these goals? Recognizing this as a target and making this a reality, however, are two entirely different things. To achieve these goals, training centers must fundamentally alter the ways in which they function and mentor young minds.[5]

Institutional Reorganization

First of all, academic centers will need to reorganize themselves into flexible, friendly, cooperative healthcare institutions prepared to enter the twenty-first century. This reorganization will be very difficult for organizations that were designed to function more like European-style universities of the last century than the multimillion-dollar healthcare giants that they have become. The old days of inefficiency will need to give way to an entirely new organization filled with enthusiasm for new processes and entrepreneurial spirit.

Adopting new management policies and decentralizing decision-making processes are essential to the evolution of any academic institution. Yet many places continue to resist these changes in favor of an old-style management philosophy of holding all of the decision-making power in the hands of a few people at the top. This dysfunctional structure has several destructive results but most important is the tremendous delay in responding to new opportunities and challenges. As management guru Tom Peters has clearly pointed out in his book, *Thriving on Chaos*, organizations can no longer afford the delay that occurs when only a few people within an organization are empowered to make decisions.[6]

Universities should be leading the management revolution by adopting policies that fully utilize the potential of all employees, rather than just the chosen few at the top. Those institutions that choose this path could unleash the creative potential of thousands of our country's brightest people. This change would result in renewed growth and development of the university and would serve as a beacon of organizational light to all who train there. In addition, other institutions throughout the country would be influenced by the university's creativity and success.

This reengineering would be extremely difficult for some training institutions. The primary leadership paradigm in many programs is acquiring and hoarding power. Power is the primary currency in academia, and unfortunately it is completely misunderstood. Many people act as if there is a shortage of power and guard it jealously. However, truly successful managers have discovered just the opposite. By bringing others into the fold and sharing power with them, the leader's position and strength are actually enhanced. It is only in refusing to share power that a shortage develops. The power bases at some universities have been amassed over years and will not willingly be surrendered. It will take tremendous courage and leadership to resurrect the long-dormant potential of teaching centers. Without this type of unwavering commitment, however, some academic centers face the possibility of closing their doors. Academic institutions may not yet be aware of this threat or be willing to undertake the difficult and painful work of re-inventing themselves, but there really is no other alternative.

Cooperation

The requirement for cooperation among various disciplines and departments also will require a complete restructuring in training centers. Some centers serve as models for interdisciplinary cooperation and work. In these programs, professionals from different backgrounds work cooperatively to better serve the institution, promote research, enhance education, and most importantly, provide world-class behavioral healthcare for their patients. Unfortunately, at many teaching centers this type of cooperation is but a dim possibility. In these institutions, deep rivalries divide the disciplines. An unspoken hierarchy determines the pecking order and the staff are powerless to escape it. Competition and intellectual snobbery are the order of the day. This atmosphere creates a poisoned work environment that prevents the kind of creative synergy that could result from bringing together people from different backgrounds.

An additional problem unrelated to specific training backgrounds results from a lack of cooperation among different departments. Again, some institutions are models of cooperation. All parts of these hospitals are focused on the overall mission and constantly seek out ways to improve their overall functioning. Unfortunately, all too many training sites are divided into functional chimneys with little understanding of or interest in the overall success of the institution. Rather than seeing themselves as part of a large organization focused on teaching, research, and the efficient delivery of unparalleled quality healthcare, they narrowly define their work within their area. In this model, workers have no appreciation of their contributions to the overall mission. After all, they are just receptionists, maintenance persons, or housekeepers. Their main goal is to stay out of trouble and minimize their work for that day (this is especially common in environments where there is no reward for outstanding service and no consequence for failure).

In order for institutions to thrive in today's climate, all employees at every level must be committed to efficient work processes and high-quality outcomes, not just the narrow completion of their minimum job requirements. No matter what field they are in, the front-runners in every industry have a workforce committed to the company's products and their success. However, if people feel that they are just putting in their eight hours each day, the organization will soon be eclipsed by those who know how to motivate and empower their employees.

Interfacing effectively with outside agencies (e.g., community mental health centers, referral hospitals, outside clinicians, and other organizations) is also important. Although some training centers handle these interfaces perfectly, others treat outsiders with disdain and look down from their "ivory towers" on the rest of the healthcare system. These attitudes must be changed in order for training centers to take their proper place in the healthcare community. This model of cooperation also will serve as a powerful influence on all trainees who witness it.

Cost

Teaching centers have had trouble competing in the area of cost. Under the old "cost-based" method of reimbursement, inefficiency and excessive charges were rewarded. Academic behavioral health programs will need to "re-invent" themselves with regard to overhead and overall costs. Some research centers point to the high cost of research as an added factor in their price, yet we are all aware of well-publicized reports of research "overhead" being spent on things that have nothing to do with education and research.

The entire culture of some organizations must change in order for academia to fully participate in the next generation of healthcare delivery. All too many teaching centers have some form of "guaranteed employment" (for faculty as well as staff members). To ensure the future success of academia, these centers must move to incentive plans through which all employees have a stake in the success of the institution. Only by tapping the creative energy of their entire institution will training and research centers become efficient, well-functioning healthcare delivery systems. The alternative is to watch more aggressive and focused organizations pass them by and perhaps make academic institutions irrelevant to the future of behavioral health.

Academic institutions could serve as a benchmark for others in terms of cost and efficiency. By focusing their powerful research tools and academic prowess on the inefficiencies within their organizations, they could experiment with new management strategies and serve as a model for all of their trainees in this area. Unfortunately, some academicians pride themselves on their lack of concern for cost. They believe that this indifference to price places them above other clinicians somehow. I believe this lack of concern is unconscionable in an era of scarce resources and is one of the factors that has precipitated our current healthcare crisis. Academia can and should set the standard for high-quality, low-cost care and this model would, in turn, influence all clinicians who trained there.

However, there will have to be some change in our current unofficial national policy of letting the care of the uninsured (and the underinsured) fall so heavily on the shoulders of the academic community. We cannot ask our training institutions to compete on cost when we also ask them to care for so many without reimbursement. Our country's unwillingness to provide for the healthcare needs of some of our fellow citizens cannot continue. It is both inhumane and shortsighted. In addition, the threat to the financial survival of our academic institutions also threatens our future supply of behavioral health clinicians.

Some have suggested that a tax on all MCOs may be a solution to funding healthcare research and training. This proposal has some merit and would help contribute to an important community need. However, I would be strongly opposed to further subsidizing the current inefficiency that exists throughout much of academia without some demonstration of a commitment to change on the part of the institutions that would benefit.

Opportunities for Collaboration

There exists a great potential for mutual benefit from collaborative efforts between MCOs and training institutions. It will not be possible for our current healthcare delivery model to be viable much longer. A new paradigm based solely on financial principles will also fail. What then is to become our new model for delivering high-quality, low-cost care in a "patient-friendly" way? Although this new model has yet to be determined, the task of developing it will require tremendous talent and energy (not to mention ongoing research and refinement). The solution to our healthcare crisis may be a partnership between MCOs and training institutions that does not focus on either "keeping the beds full" or limiting access to behavioral healthcare services as much as possible. By combining some of the finest researchers and clinicians in the world with newly developed healthcare financing and delivery systems, we may be able to find workable solutions to what now seem to be unsolvable problems. A partnership such as this would require great courage on both sides as well as bold imaginative leadership and a willingness to surrender some control. In exchange, we may have the necessary synergy that will be required to go forward into the twenty-first century with the kind of healthcare system that works for everyone, not just for the people who can afford it.

Notes

1. Sternbach, K. O., & Waters, R. (1995). Anatomy of a Medicaid behavioral managed care program: Green Spring's Advo-Care of Tennessee. *Behavioral Health Management, 15*, 13–24.
2. Eisenberg, J. M. (1986). *Doctors' decisions and the cost of medical care.* Ann Arbor, MI: Health Administration Press Perspectives, p. 3.
3. Doyle, E. (1995, April). Preparing residents for the real (managed care) world. *American College of Physicians Observer*, p. 11.
4. Wildavsky, A. (1977). Doing better and feeling worse: The political pathology of health policy. In J. Knowles (Ed.), *Doing better and feeling worse: Health in the United States* (pp. 105–123). New York: Norton.
5. Beigel, A., & Santiago, J. M. (1995). Redefining the general psychiatrist: Values, reforms and issues for psychiatric residency education. *Psychiatric Services, 46*, 769–774.
6. Peters, T. (1987). *Thriving on Chaos.* New York: Knopf, pp. 281–389.

Chapter Nine

Continuing Education in the Managed Care Era

Deborah A. Teplow

The account that Dr. Schuster offers in the Introduction parallels my own experience. He reflects on his reaction to hospital practice from the context of the competitive real estate enterprise in which he had worked before medical school. He uses the words "astounded" and "surprised" to describe his initial responses to what he experienced: healthcare systems willing to sacrifice patients' interests in effective, efficient care for providers' interests in convenience and financial benefit; enterprises that thrived in spite of customer-*un*friendly practices; and medical care seemingly "immune from the rules of classic economics."

Since 1993, I have been actively involved in the development and delivery of continuing education (CE) and continuing medical education (CME) of behavioral healthcare providers throughout the United States. As executive director of the Institute for Behavioral Healthcare and the director of CE/CME, my job has been to ensure that the institute's training adequately prepares providers to deliver care within the prevailing systems of care. Since launching our first series of courses focused on care delivery within a managed care environment, I have observed profound shifts in provider knowledge and attitudes. Common responses on needs assessment surveys that asked clinicians to identify topics of interest for further training often included statements like, "Teach me how to continue in solo private practice and avoid managed care." Questions from participants in courses on diagnosis and treatment planning reflected marked ignorance about the fundamental paradigm shift taking place. It was common in those "ancient days" to hear questions about how to code traditional open-ended approaches to treatment in such a way that managed care would pay, rather than how to employ managed care–friendly approaches.

Over the past three years, general clinician attitudes reflected in comments at courses and in paper surveys appear to have shifted. They now range from grudging acceptance of what appears inevitable to a welcome embrace of the managed care values of best practices, demonstrated outcomes, population-based care, collaborative approaches to care, and accountability. Clearly, a tremendous amount of work remains to be done to demonstrate and convince providers of managed care's ability to deliver quality patient care. However, providers in 1996 appear more willing to consider alternatives than they were just a few years ago.

The Current Climate

Many issues confront academic institutions and professional schools that now must grapple with the impact healthcare restructuring is having on American healthcare delivery and the implications restructuring has for clinical training. As new models of healthcare delivery evolve, traditional training programs are being forced to address fundamental and operational issues to ensure both their viability and relevance. They must articulate a new notion of mission, purpose, and goals that reconciles market-driven interests with strongly held transcendental values embodied by academia regarding scientific inquiry and intellectual pursuit.

For organizations charged with delivering continuing educational activities to practicing healthcare providers, the issues are somewhat different. Whereas academic training programs face challenges to their fundamental policies and processes, their "audience" of neophytes comes relatively fresh and unencumbered, seeking entree into a new area of endeavor. The audience for continuing education is vastly different, however. It consists of established practitioners who, in many cases, come with a store-house of knowledge derived from decades of practical experience. Not only must providers of continuing education activities concern themselves with the task of retraining practitioners previously trained in approaches often antithetical to current managed care practice, but they must cope with a distinctly resistant and some-times hostile learner cohort.

This chapter will delineate some of the challenges and oppor-tunities facing professionals and decision makers responsible for the continuing professional development of managed care providers. It will summarize the current requirements, standards, and programs for CE/CME for behavioral healthcare professionals; provide an assessment of the value of traditional CE/CME for providers and managed care organizations (MCOs); describe challenges facing providers and MCOs; delineate areas of opportunity for improve-ment in traditional approaches to CE/CME; and offer case studies of new approaches to CE/CME which promise to address the spe-cific needs of MCOs and their providers.

Managed Care and Traditional CE/CME

Postgraduate professional education traditionally has been one of the foremost mechanisms by which clinicians retain currency with scientific research, new theoretical knowledge, and innovations in clinical practice. Today, documented evidence of participation in CE/CME activities is required to become licensed by state organi-zations governing professional practice; maintain hospital staff priv-ileges; retain membership in professional associations and medical and professional societies; or purchase professional liability insur-ance at favorable rates. Lack of national standardization and the exertion of local authority with respect to the requirements for each professional group, however, are failings of the current system. CE/CME requirements vary profoundly from state to state and pro-fession to profession. These variations are evident in the number of hours and frequency of training required, the kind of educational activities recognized as valid for CE/CME, and credit designations, training formats, and content.

Establishing Appropriate Standards

Traditional CE/CME criteria, standards, and guidelines for program development have been published by all regulatory organizations to ensure that courses designated for CE/CME credit meet acceptable standards for educational quality. In today's environment, however, the exacting standards don't necessarily provide the same essential measure of quality that is being established through emerging data- and outcomes-driven approaches being applied in critical areas of healthcare delivery. For CE/CME to be of greatest service to the entire healthcare community, including managed care, much more attention must be paid to establishing criteria, standards, and mechanisms for measuring educational outcomes to better reflect the realities of service delivery in this era of managed care.

Just as clinical processes today are subject to evaluation for efficacy and cost-effectiveness, so too must the educational processes prescribed for the continuing professional development of healthcare providers be subject to standards of accountability. Boards and professional associations that are unresponsive to the demands of today's healthcare marketplace or slow to adapt do a disservice to the practitioners whose professional development they are charged with guiding. Ultimately, they do a disservice to consumers, too, for consumers depend on the rapid response of healthcare providers to the changing standards of care to ensure that they receive adequate, appropriate, and effective care.

For MCOs, the continuing professional development of their providers is of vital importance. Professional education and training must not only help providers maintain currency with state-of-the-art approaches to care and care management, but they must also be able to achieve much more fundamental goals of establishing new knowledge bases and skill sets and inculcating new attitudes and values among clinicians who are not yet managed care "savvy."

Enhancing CE/CME's Traditional Role

Today, MCOs employ rather traditional training modalities to accommodate the diverse learning needs of their providers while limiting costs. Many offer general orientation training for new providers, in-house intensive workshops that last from one day to several days for clinical directors and case managers, fully or partially subsidized external training for staff providers or preferred providers, and independent study modules in the form of audiotapes and videotapes and workbooks. Follow-up activities may include discussions, presentations to other staff members, and telephone conferences. So far, little work has been done to establish and improve competencies, measure outcomes, or link training with changes in practice patterns. As MCOs develop more sophisticated data collection and provider profiling processes, some of these elements of provider CE/CME may be taken into account.

Consideration of participation in traditional CE/CME activities constitutes one element of the data collected by MCOs in the provider credentialing and profiling process. In fact, most MCOs account for the formal CE activities of their providers—outside of initial orientation training—solely by relying on the credentialing and licensing requirements of external organizations (such as state licensing boards) that govern the professional practice of specific provider cohorts. This is clearly just a first step in formulating a serviceable managed care philosophy and approach to continuing professional development. Traditional external controls do not ensure that current educational interventions improve the quality of provider services because of

- The absence of CE/CME requirements for a significant number of clinicians

- The variability in requirements for those whose boards require it
- The absence of a comprehensive curriculum that addresses issues specific to managed care
- The lack of adequate mechanisms to account for quality and outcomes

Significant improvements in the structure of CE/CME could be made through collaboration among CE/CME regulatory organizations, professional associations, and MCOs. In a productive partnership, CE/CME organizations could provide expertise in educational program oversight, provider evaluation and licensing, and management of specific provider cohorts. Managed care would be an agent for the consumer/purchaser by translating the demands of the marketplace into the context of service delivery, direct and indirect patient care, and care management. Managed care would also contribute its developing sophistication in effective data collection and outcomes measurement to establish reliable systems to evaluate the real-world application of educational interventions.

Updating the Curriculum for Managed Care

Traditional CE/CME does not offer or require a comprehensive curriculum designed to adequately retrain clinicians in managed care practice. Traditional CE/CME has concerned itself with improving and enhancing provider knowledge and skills within the context of the prevailing fee-for-service delivery system. Within this system, introducing new practice processes and concepts was a process of building on a pre-existing and firmly established foundation of practice that was relevant and valued by the system. Today, CE/CME providers must reconsider and redefine the educational tasks they must undertake. They can no longer think in terms of promoting incremental change. Rather, CE/CME providers must be able to direct major retraining efforts that not only produce activities to increase knowledge and develop skills, but also replace fundamental and outdated concepts and values with newer ones that more appropriately meet the demands of the prevailing healthcare environment. For behavioral healthcare providers, this means access to courses never before considered essential or relevant, such as practice management, computerization, marketing, or record keeping.

A new recognition of the urgency of including topics on the "business of healthcare" is reflected in CME guidelines published recently by the American Academy of Family Physicians (AAFP, 1995). The AAFP requires their members to take courses that "Have a direct bearing on family physicians' ability to deliver patient care including, but not limited to, laboratory regulations, managed care/practice management, utilization review/quality assurance, coding."

It further defines its philosophy in an addendum to the stated requirements:

> The AAFP Commission on Continuing Medical Education considers practice management topics to be important for all aspects of a physician's medical practice. These topics may vary with geographic location and socioeconomic trends in a given area. Maintaining a viable, cost-effective, efficient practice is vital. Physicians must be informed on the broader aspect of the "business of medicine" in order to be accountable to their patients and to maintain a viable practice.

Other associations and regulatory boards would better serve their constituents if they, too, included recommendations for education in these topical areas.

A sample managed care curriculum for retraining behavioral healthcare practitioners across disciplines might include
- Practice management
- Administration

- Staffing
- Fiscal management and budgeting
- Office management
- Insurance intake
- Claims
- Information systems
- Computerized office management applications
- Computerized treatment planning intake, assessment, and documentation
- Clinical skills
- Assessment, diagnosis, and treatment planning
- Psychotherapy (brief therapy approaches, triage, and groups)
- Providing a continuum of care: matching the severity of illness with the intensity of service
- Working productively in interdisciplinary teams
- Integration with primary care
- Collaborating with case managers
- Drawing on community resources
- Using clinical guidelines
- Communication and documentation
- Outcomes measurement
- Quality management
- Ethical concerns
- Confidentiality
- Multiparity nature of managed care
- Electronic transmission and communication issues
- Local, state, and federal regulations

- Informed consent
- Legal ramifications
- Business principles
- Assuming and managing risk
- Benefit design
- Insurance industry structure and functions
- Pricing and promotion
- Organizational development

(David Nace, M.D., personal communication, 1995)

Conflicting Goals and Objectives

The goals, objectives, and fundamental values inculcated by training programs that prepared most of today's practicing clinicians for an unregulated fee-for-service system are at direct odds with those of managed care. For clinicians who are just entering training, the values reflected by managed care are consonant with those in other sectors, such as business, education, and entertainment. Market-driven economics, accountability, quality management, customer service, data-driven decision making, standardization, and demonstrated outcomes, are essential values reflected in virtually every aspect of modern endeavor. Although trainees may not have anticipated finding these values expressed in the "soft sciences" and helping professions, they have been familiar concepts whose impact has already been felt on college campuses for many years. For older clinicians, however, these values are anathema to strongly held beliefs developed over years of practice. What has appealed to older, experienced clinicians as the "art of therapy" is becoming too much like business, consumed by attention to the bottom line.

Table 9.1 shows some of the most commonly cited differences between traditional and managed behavioral healthcare approaches.[1]

Table 9.1. Traditional and Managed Behavioral Healthcare Approaches to Therapy.

Traditional	*Managed Care*
Presenting problems indicate more basic pathology requiring therapeutic attention	Presenting problems are initial focus of attention. Focus is on identifying specific problems, strengths, and resources
Therapy consists of open-ended exploration of many issues and problems to uncover underlying sources of psychopathology	Therapy is highly structured and goal oriented; every session achieves tangible objectives to move client quickly to achieving overall treatment goals
Treatment is as complete, thorough, and comprehensive as possible	Treatment provides least intensive, least invasive intervention in least restrictive setting
Goal is a once-and-for-all "cure" and a change in basic character	Goals are symptom reduction, reversal of impairment, and restoration of baseline functioning. Goals are modest, limited, and achievable, and demonstrated by objective measurements
Therapy requires a long-term approach to achieve lasting psychological change	Therapy is provided as an intermittent service, addressing crucial developmental issues throughout the life cycle
Therapist is a passive interpreter	Therapist is active and directive
Change occurs only in the context of the treatment session	Gains during sessions are reinforced by adjunctive resources including homework, groups, and 12-step programs
Therapeutic relationship is maintained as patient changes	Acceptance that significant change can occur after treatment; it does not have to be witnessed by therapist
Recognizes fiscal reward for retaining patients in treatment	Conscious of fiscal issues and protects resources

Considers client the only customer	Recognizes that the customer is both the client and the payer/purchaser
Views patient's treatment as the most important	Views patient's activity in the world as the most important aspect of patient's life
Therapist assumes responsibility for patients in care at the moment	Therapist is part of a coordinated system of care responsible for the health status of a defined population
Treatment is based on the intuitive judgment of the clinician	Treatment is a collaboration between clinician and patient, based on practice guidelines to ensure consistency of care and the most appropriate choice of treatment options
Clinical processes are determined by individualized judgments and local practice customs	Clinical processes are informed by objective outcomes data

Source: Adapted from Winegar & Bistline, 1994; Browning & Browning, 1994; Hoyt, 1995; Sederer & Dickey, 1996; and Chrisman, 1995.

Resistance to Retraining

CE/CME planners could develop effective programs by taking into account the profound differences between the values and beliefs that characterize traditional approaches to care (from training five or more years ago) and those of managed care. There is little data, however, to inform us about how to conduct major retraining of the diverse professions represented in behavioral healthcare. Some light may be shed on the issue by reviewing the little research that has been conducted on retraining medical specialists for primary care practice.

An article published in 1995 addresses physicians' career choices and their attitudes toward retraining for primary care. The study asked questions regarding their motivation for choosing their specialties, their satisfaction with working as specialists, and their feelings about the potential need to retrain. The concept of retraining elicited strong negative reactions. The key themes that emerged were

- Retraining feels punitive, as if the work to which specialists have devoted their careers was somehow flawed.
- Retraining is profoundly demoralizing because specialists perceive that they are being denied the opportunity to do what they like to do and what they want to do.
- Specialty practice is intellectually more challenging and satisfying and more interesting clinically.
- Specialists chose their fields for the unique features of the specialty, the specific skill set the specialty required, and for a "fit" with attitudes and personalities.

Although the study was limited in focus to internal medicine subspecialists, and their issues may differ from other subspecialties or disciplines, some of the themes may be valuable to consider for retraining behavioral healthcare practitioners for managed care. Perhaps the most important theme to address is that of "fit."

Extrapolating from the material in Table 9.1, it's realistic to suggest that the clinician who five or more years ago found behavioral healthcare an appealing career choice would value autonomy, intensive work over a long duration, ongoing relationships with patients featuring regular and frequent contact, choice regarding professional collaboration, unstructured processes, lack of demand for organizational or business management, no requirement to operationalize his or her decisions, and a relatively high salary. What appeal does managed care hold for such a clinician, and how good is the fit?

Perhaps one of the most valuable services CE/CME planners could provide would be a program to enable clinicians to critically examine the factors associated with career choices and retraining. The postmodern notion of transferable skills and values-based career choice could be called into play by identifying those skills and values for which there may still be an appropriate fit in a managed care setting.

Clinician Response to the Paradigm Shift

What is referred to as a "paradigm shift" in the unfolding of healthcare restructuring is experienced by clinicians as a cataclysmic wrenching apart of systems and approaches to care in which they enjoyed significant professional success and recognition and rewarding financial remuneration.

Many practitioners resent the intrusion of managed care, and believe that it imposes almost intolerable limitations and restrictions on the ways they have conducted successful practices for the entirety of their professional lives. Their negative reactions to managed care can seriously inhibit successful retraining efforts.

CE/CME providers and MCOs offering retraining courses often encounter practitioners who exhibit resistance, resentment, anger, and confusion. Recognizing the stages many practitioners experience in reconciling themselves fully to the reality of managed care may help educators address practitioners' specific needs.

Several writers make reference to Kubler-Ross's four-stage process—denial, anger, bargaining, and acceptance—which clinicians experience as a result of managed care's impact on their practices. Some practitioners attempt to deny that managed care will affect their practices. They consider that negative patient outcomes and patient dissatisfaction with managed care services will stimulate a return to traditional models of care. Those at the anger stage take up a battle cry of poor quality, inappropriate or inadequate care, or unethical practices. In the bargaining stages, practitioners concede the need to join a managed care network, but attempt to continue practicing in the "old" ways by manipulating the system for added therapy sessions or increased numbers of inpatient days. Practitioners who reach the stage of acceptance pursue partnerships with managed care to deliver the best quality care within the constraints of limited resources.

In our experience at the institute, trainers can help clinicians reconcile themselves to the changes facing them by giving managed care a "human" face. Trainers who can share their own frustrations and concerns about the shifts taking place in healthcare, admit the problems and limitations of managed care's current stage of development, and articulate a vision for care that emphasizes quality of patient outcome rather than cost can influence providers' abilities to accept the change. In addition to providing a responsive sounding board and an appealing model exemplified by honesty and personal integrity, tangible evidence of managed care–friendly approaches contributes significantly to increasing providers' willingness to accommodate these momentous changes. Some of the most compelling "arguments" for time-efficient approaches come in the form of role plays by expert clinicians and videotapes illustrating new approaches to assessment and treatment. "A picture is worth a thousand words" is a useful adage in this context.

Special Requirements for Provider Retraining

Retraining requires unique approaches that are not part of traditional CE/CME activities. Traditional CE/CME activities are usually offered as a "one-shot deal" in the form of a seminar lasting from one to several days, a multiple-day conference, or a series of self-contained presentations such as grand rounds or other case conferences. Effective retraining requires more extensive exposure to new materials, opportunities for rehearsal of new skills, and feedback.

Results from research studies suggest several ways to promote positive changes in provider behaviors. These results indicate that CE/CME should encourage self-reflection, self-critique, and critical evaluation of new ideas and techniques.[2] The capacity for and ongoing practice of critical self-assessment and self-audit will enable well-trained clinicians whose practice patterns and values are aligned with managed care to self-manage rather than be managed by external agents such as case managers and reviewers.

Ways to Enhance Retraining

Modeling

In choosing CME courses from among a range of choices, physicians preferred to attend those taught by experts. In addition to feeling confident that they would receive cutting-edge information of significant depth and breadth, the physicians wanted to observe the decision-making processes of the experts. Effective retraining provides adequate exposure to experts who can model and articulate the thinking processes they use in carrying out their professional responsibilities.

In a recent study on physician compliance with newly established practice guidelines, researchers found that physician adoption was markedly improved through fostering opinion leaders.[3]

Consultation

Opportunities for intensive, one-to-one discussions with a consultant who is viewed by the learner as competent and credible promote striking and consistent performance improvement, especially when the contact is designed to remedy knowledge deficiencies, as in the case of retraining.[4]

Reinforcement

Changes in clinical behavior are enhanced through reinforcement mechanisms that include computer-generated reminders, office reminder techniques, consultation with peers and reviewers, and opportunities to discuss practice issues at a local level with peers who understand the unique characteristics of practice.

Instructional Design

The best short-term knowledge gains and greatest retention of new material are facilitated by actively engaging the learner, narrowly defining the subject area, providing experiential exercises, and organizing the material around a specific clinical problem.

Self-Assessment

Opportunities to participate in chart audits or to compare individual practice pattern data with that of peers also offer demonstrated benefits for retraining efforts. Clinicians are sensitive to self-perceptions about their status in their own community of practice and vulnerable to data that places them outside established local standards.

Learning Logs

Logs that clinicians use to record their ongoing learning through formal CE/CME activities, consultation, reading of professional journals and other materials, participation as teachers or supervisors, and informal discussions with colleagues can help clarify, amplify, and verify new understanding and insights.

Current Funding Strategies

Funding of training is yet another challenge for both managed care companies and providers. Most large companies offer their providers a variety of ways to receive at least some training at no cost. Many offer in-house orientation training for their new providers. This training covers topics such as company philosophy and operations, utilization review, quality management, and various aspects of brief therapy. In addition, companies offer free training on topics for which they perceive a deficiency among their providers or which they are obligated to provide by contract with purchasers. For example, a purchaser concerned with substance abuse may require the company to provide a certain number of hours of training on that topic to those providers servicing the contract. In addition, requirements by accrediting agencies also prompt companies to offer training to the provider community for modest and affordable fees.

To encourage their providers to participate in external CE/CME activities, some companies offer their providers various incentives including training stipends or subsidized training. For example, members of the Institute for Behavioral Healthcare's Consortium for Clinical Excellence, who are drawn from leading MCOs in the country, contribute some of their training resources to make a wide range of training topics relevant to managed care practice available to their providers at significantly reduced costs in cities across the country.

Training stipends most often are designated primarily for the cost of tuition with a very modest amount, if any, allowed for travel and lodging. These additional costs usually must be borne by providers themselves. In addition, over the last few years, the availability of stipend support has been reduced, and the amount now ranges from about $200 to $500. Organizations also control costs by opting to send fewer representatives, and they require those who do attend training to share their information with their colleagues through presentations, copies of notes, or consultation.

Even generous in-house training and various arrangements for subsidized external training can cost providers, however. Sometimes, the cost for in-house training is shared with the provider. When cost is shared, the provider may have to pay for either a modest participation fee or for a certain component of the training, such as the cost for the processing of CE/CME credit. Finally, in addition to the expense of paying for nontuition-related costs, providers must also forgo the revenues they would ordinarily earn by being in the office seeing clients.

Although these endeavors by MCOs may help orient and advance providers' knowledge to some extent, they do not provide enough opportunity for reflection, rehearsal, and reinforcement that thorough retraining demands. Providers must pursue these opportunities on their own and at a significant cost.

Opportunities for the New Millennium

There is no question that CE/CME activities will change significantly within the next five to ten years. Considerations of cost for travel, tuition, and lodging; insistence on access to the most up-to-date information; convenience of scheduling, preference for learning environment; and the demand for and expectation of individually tailored professional development activities all point toward profound changes in the CE/CME landscape and the increased use of alternative forms of training delivery.

Future Funding Challenges

Provider CE/CME in the future will undoubtedly be shaped by three factors which, in the era of expanding managed care, are taking on more compelling importance: cost, outcomes, and technology. The costs associated with traditional CE/CME include tuition, travel, lodging, and lost wages from being absent from the office for several hours to several days. These costs are becoming increasingly burdensome and untenable for clinicians to assume by themselves or for MCOs to subsidize. The cost of time away from family and the pursuit of other personal interests also affect providers' attitudes toward professional development.

In the new millennium, funding of traditional CE/CME will be problematic because the demand for training will increase without an accompanying rise in available funds to pay for it. As it stands now, providers will bear the brunt of the burden. They will have to subsidize training just to fulfill their licensing requirements as state organizations increase CE/CME requirements and introduce new mandatory CE/CME for professional groups who don't yet have any. In addition, productive and rewarding participation as a managed care provider will entail continuous and focused training to retain currency with practice management and clinical skills, because MCOs will continue to develop general approaches to care, treatment guidelines, standardized documentation processes, and outcomes measurement tools and processes. The challenge for producers of CE/CME activities will be to address and accommodate increasing demands for training with the ever-tightening resources.

Increasing Demands for Demonstrated Outcomes

Today, outcomes measurement of educational interventions is in a fledgling state. The most common measurements employed by producers of traditional CE/CME are the pretest and posttest. These tests may measure how much knowledge the learner has gained within the course of the training, but they don't account for long-term retention, how the learner puts the new knowledge or skills into play in his or her professional practice, or how the newly gained knowledge or skills affect patient care. In the future, educators will develop ways to account more accurately for the results of their training interventions. A first step toward this goal will be a way to measure baseline competencies against which to measure demonstrable posttraining skills at various intervals. For managed care companies concerned with developing cohorts of highly effective providers, the ability to measure provider competency and the effectiveness of the training they subsidize is already of great interest.

Technology and Training

Technology will advance the response capacity of CE/CME producers to deliver a range of just-in-time learning opportunities at reasonable cost to clinicians. Historically, alternatives to classroom instruction have included home study, text-based modules, and audiotaped or videotaped presentations. These low-tech media have provided clinicians with the core benefits of distance learning modalities: convenience, relative low cost, and readily accessible information. Another appeal of many home study modules has been the opportunity to earn CE/CME credit that could satisfy licensure requirements.

Today's evolving technology offers increasingly dynamic and effective education and training opportunities. Although telemedicine has been used successfully for many years, especially to train physicians in highly technical clinical areas, its convenience, cost, and accessibility have made it unfeasible for all but large hospitals or academic medical centers. With the advancement and improvement of Internet technology, clinicians may now take advantage of distance learning and communications opportunities for very modest costs in ways that are completely tailored to the needs of particular uses. Among the modalities available today are text-based CE/CME on-line, interactive CD-ROM, telephonic conferencing, and video conferencing.[5]

Paul Engstrom, editor of a new monthly serial *Medicine on the Net*, writes, "The Net, if you exploit its potential, may well be the most powerful, convenient, easy-to-use tool at your grasp for assessing the good, the bad, and the ugly in prepaid healthcare."[6]

Technological alternatives now available or under development include on-line consultation, electronic discussion forums, video conferencing, text-based interactive instruction, simulations, journal clubs, live-stream audio and video, and interactive multimedia. These media will enable practitioners to access a huge array of information resources including published journals, news articles, technical reports, and research data. They will also be able to contact experts and other colleagues around the world to engage in ongoing interactive discussions and conduct research. In addition to the educational benefits that providers may derive from these emerging technologies, the providers may also utilize these advancements to offer patient education materials to the public or to select groups by employing easy-to-use development and authoring tools.

In the past, several factors inhibited providers from using electronic communications. These factors included lack of available or procurable computer systems, lack of time to learn the applications, perceived lack of real benefit or relevance, resistance to the use of computers in a discipline that prizes human interface, lack of typing skill, and general anxiety about computer literacy.[7] The explosion of easy-to-use point-and-click technologies, widespread adoption of computers in all facets of work and home activities, and easy access to a plethora of professional healthcare information make technological solutions more attractive, less alien, and less daunting to providers. To be sure, healthcare providers have not been among the first professionals to embrace this technology, and older providers may maintain their resistance longer than younger professionals. However, providers just entering the field are already accustomed to using computers for carrying out a diverse range of transactions. Older providers may gain entry to computer use through a networked on-line catalogue at the public library or through conversion of their practice management systems from paper- to computer-based systems.

Electronic Discussion Forums

Electronic discussion forums, referred to as newsgroups or usergroups, offer focused discussion on specific topics of interest to the subscriber group and provide a unique and valuable source of up-to-date information from peers. Reading the entries lets a participant identify issues of current concern and amass a sampling of diverse perspectives on a specific topic. Some users express concern regarding the veracity of the information presented on-line. Although it is impossible to establish the quality of the information contributors offer, reading and participating in the discussion can stimulate providers' thinking about critical issues and provide a context for understanding trends in the profession.

To participate in a newsgroup, the user sends an e-mail request to the discussion group manager ("list owner"). Once on the list, a user will receive all messages sent to the list from other members on the list, and he or she can participate in the discussion by sending replies to the address designated for the list. It is common for lists to feature discussion on several ongoing topics depending on the participants' interests. In addition to offering a venue for open and spontaneous discussion, newsgroups enable participants to get hard-to-find or esoteric information from peers by allowing them to post inquiries to the list. It is common to read questions that begin, "Does anyone know . . . ?" or "I'm considering using xyz. Has anyone had experience with this?"

Since 1994, the Institute for Behavioral Healthcare has run a continuous discussion forum devoted to discussions on managed behavioral healthcare. Topics under discussion have included treatment approaches for specific disorders, outcomes measurement, criteria for using group psychotherapy, healthcare financing, contract negotiation, issues providers have with particular MCOs, and announcements of upcoming training.

Comprehensive Resource Sites

Many World Wide Web sites offer a full complement of resources including news and industry updates, full-length articles, reference materials, CE/CME modules, extensive links to related sites, and discussion groups devoted to specific issues. One such site is Behavior OnLine (Internet address: http://www.behavior.net). Behavior OnLine is an excellent example of an interactive, text-based Web site. Founded by psychologists John M. Grohol and Gilbert Levin, the site includes in-depth interviews of leading clinicians and interactive discussions generated by the interviews; on-line CE/CME activities; calendar listings of behavioral healthcare training across the country, many specifically applicable to managed care practice; a "virtual" behavioral healthcare bookstore offering e-mail book purchasing; and descriptions of behavioral health-related organizations.

Text-Based Interactive Instruction

CE/CME has been available for at least a few years as text-based modules consisting of a course outline, written text, bibliographic references, and a quiz that the reader sends to the sponsoring organization to receive credit. As the technology becomes easier to use, more and more CE/CME modules are becoming interactive. At the minimum, most CE/CME now contains hypertext that allows the user to click on specific words in the text to go to linked pages for additional information. For example, a user may click on the name of the author to read a complete biography or the author's publications list. Hypertext links may also provide definitions of specific terms, tables, references, lab results, or other relevant information. Hypertext may also be used to offer hints on quiz questions to prompt or clarify the reader's thinking on a particular question.

More comprehensive text-based interactive instructional modules allow the user to post comments or questions to the author/instructor or to other readers. This communication can be sent privately or publicly for anyone to read or to which anyone may respond. Several producers of such modules then make the discussion available to all readers.

Text-based CE for nurses may be found at Nightingale, a nursing site maintained by the University of Tennessee. In addition to its selection of on-line CE courses in general medicine, it often features a few courses of relevance to nurses who are practicing in behavioral healthcare. Examples of courses offered in 1996 include treatment of survivors of incest and managing behavioral complications of dementia. Nightingale can be accessed at gopher://nightingale.con.utk.edu:70/00/Education/Continuing.

Physicians and other providers who are interested in CME can subscribe to a list that notifies them of Web sites offering CME activities. To subscribe to the Continuing Medical Education Mail List, you may send the message "subscribe CME-L" to listserv@listserv.net.

Journals

Journals are now available on-line or on CD-ROM. The CD-ROM format provides text, color photos, sound, illustrations, and movie sequences. It also offers sophisticated search routines to locate articles, specific techniques, and references, as well as quizzes and other interactive exercises. Journals on CD-ROM include the *New England Journal of Medicine*, which offers 312 issues on two disks, and the *American Family Physician*.

In addition to CD-ROM, electronic publication of professional journals is also available on-line. These professional journals not only reflect local or national perspectives, but enable clinicians to communicate with colleagues worldwide on a broad range of issues. *Psychiatry On-Line*, which was launched in 1994, claims to be the first fully electronic medical journal. It is one example of how Internet technology can facilitate global communications among clinicians by making current research and professional communications available. This international, independent, free, peer-reviewed journal is available solely through the Internet's World Wide Web.

Mental Health Net, sponsored by CMHC Systems (Internet address: http://www.cmhc.com/readroom.htm) provides an on-line referred journal, *Perspectives,* and a reading room that offers news articles from other serial publications, such as the *APA Monitor*. *The InterPsych Newsletter,* another monthly on-line publication, can also be accessed through this site. *InterPsych* offers articles, information on on-line resources, announcements about current research projects, and a calendar listing international meetings and CE/CME in behavioral healthcare.

Live-Stream Audio and Video

Streaming audio and video refer to live broadcasts of audio and video materials. This technology, now in its fledgling state, enables organizations to transmit educational courses, corporate meetings, events, and news stories live without time delays to any site having access to the World Wide Web. One of the pioneering efforts is Cornell University's desktop videoconferencing system, CU-SeeMe, developed for use on common Macintosh and Windows platforms. Schools, corporations, and major training centers have put CU-SeeMe to use already, and it is used to distribute NASA TV to thousands of viewers worldwide.

Interactive Multimedia

Interactive multimedia allows the user to access information through text, audio, and graphics. A good example of an interactive multimedia application is the "Interactive Patient," which is available through the Marshall University School of Medicine. This application actually allows the "doctor" to interview the "patient" by typing in questions and receiving plausible answers to guide him or her through the diagnostic process. In addition to interviewing the patient, the application allows the clinician to conduct a physical examination using visual inspection, palpitation, and auscultation. The clinician can also retrieve results of lab tests and view X rays. Finally, the clinician chooses a diagnosis and treatment plan and sends them via e-mail for evaluation by electronic application. Response to submissions can take as little as a few minutes. The "Interactive Patient" can be found at: http://medicus.marshall.edu/medicus.htm.

As technology develops, allowing video and sound applications to be more easily and more quickly captured and distributed, it will become feasible for CE/CME producers to develop modules that enable clinicians to "interview" patients, observe them in interactions, and test various interventions. In addition, modules can be developed to illustrate best practices as demonstrated by master clinicians.

Video Conferencing

Video conferencing in the form of two-way audio and one-way video has been an established means for delivery of CME in medical schools and hospitals for several years. With the advancement of Internet technology, it will soon be possible to easily and cost-effectively engage people at several sites in face-to-face interaction through video cameras operated through their own desktop computers. This video conferencing capability will include both two-way audio and video. Students will not just be able to view instructors, but they also will be able to view and interact with each other in a virtual classroom. This technology can be employed for communications between clinicians and for patient interviews.

On-line Consultation

Periodic and ongoing consultation and supervision by experts at a distance will become more feasible, affordable, and reliable as these various distance communications technologies evolve. On-line consultation will enable providers to gain expert consultation on difficult cases, engage in collaborative projects and research, and participate in posttraining discussions with experts from whom they have received face-to-face classroom instruction.

Needs Assessment

In the new millennium, CE/CME producers can use electronic media to assess learning needs and interests cost-effectively and time-efficiently. Results of electronic needs assessment data collection, which are linked to a database application, can be easily calculated and reported. Research on the validity of adult learning theory in promoting change among healthcare providers demonstrates that engaging providers in defining and creating learning activities tailored to their unique and specific practice needs enhances the efficacy of educational interventions.[8] By employing diverse and engaging methods for gathering needs assessment data, CE/CME producers can be more certain of designing courses that respond to providers' needs.

In a pilot study conducted in 1994 among general practice and family physicians, researchers demonstrated that needs assessment surveys sent via e-mail had similar acceptance and response rates to conventional paper-and-pencil mail surveys.[9] The study suggested that the use of computerized data collection would be facilitated by increased access to computer networks and by easy-to-use user interfaces. With fairly universal access to the Internet available now to clinicians through academic centers, hospitals, and public access providers, plus the excellent user interfaces available through Web browsers, computerized needs assessment holds great promise. Not only can needs assessment be accomplished by surveying interest, but CE/CME producers can expand their needs assessment surveying by offering clinicians self-assessment surveys and certain forms of competency testing to establish learning needs.

—⚬—

Without a doubt, we are faced with both tremendous challenges and great opportunities to advance the interests in delivery of quality care by establishing and enhancing provider knowledge and skills through education and training. The limitations and restrictions discussed in this chapter—lack of appropriate standards, provider resistance, limited financial resources, and lack of coordination among organizations responsible for ongoing professional development—make the job of provider education and retraining a difficult one. The promise for the future depends on alignment and coordination among regulatory and licensing agencies, associations charged with accrediting CE and CME, MCOs that deliver care, purchasers and consumers of managed behavioral healthcare services, and providers who deliver the care. It also depends on incorporating strategic approaches to education and training already in place in other disciplines and industries; establishing well-articulated competency standards and means for testing them; employing appropriate emerging technologies; and, finally, creating supportive communities of practice that foster collaboration, mentoring, self-reflection, active engagement in all facets of needs identification, course design and implementation, and opportunities for reinforcement and recognition.

Notes

1. Winegar, N., & Bistline, J. (1994). *Marketing mental health services to managed care.* Binghamton, New York: Haworth Press; Browning, C., & Browning, B. (1994). *How to partner with managed care.* Los Angeles: Duncliff's International; Hoyt, M. (1995). *Brief therapy and managed care.* San Francisco: Jossey-Bass; Sederer, L., & Dickey, B. (1996). *Outcomes assessment in clinical practice.* Baltimore: Williams & Wilkins; Chrisman, A. (1995). How a private practitioner practices in managed care. *Journal of Psychiatry and Behavioral Health, 1*, 112–114.
2. Woolf, C. (1993). Global CHPE principles. *Journal of Continuing Education in the Health Professions, 13* (3), 229–234.
3. Lockyer, J. (1994). Clinical practice guidelines and the CME office. *Journal of Continuing Education in the Health Professions, 14* (1), 46–55.
4. Tamblyn, R., & Battista, R. (1993). Changing clinical practice: Which interventions work? *Journal of Continuing Education in the Health Professions, 13* (4), 273–288.

5. Teplow, D.A. (1996, July/August). Distance learning and just-in-time clinical education for the 21st century behavioral healthcare provider. *Behavioral Healthcare Tomorrow Journal, 5* (4).
6. Engstrom, P. (1996). Getting a grip: How the Net can help you harness managed care. *Medicine on the Net, 2,* (3), 1–5.
7. Chow, T. (1994). Bulletin board system for CME. *Journal of Continuing Education in the Health Professions, 14* (3), 166–172.
8. Scott, C. (1994). Applied adult learning theory: Broadening traditional CME programs with self-guided, computer-assisted learning. *Journal of Continuing Education in the Health Professions, 14* (2), 91–99.
9. Vanek, E., O'Connor, K., & Pomiecko, E. (1994). Using a computerized information network for assessing programming needs. *Journal of Continuing Education in the Health Professions, 14* (2), 115–118.

About the Authors

The Editors

James M. Schuster, M.D., M.B.A., is associate professor of psychiatry at Allegheny University of the Health Sciences (Pittsburgh, Pennsylvania campus). He is the director of consultation and emergency psychiatry services and director of managed care services for psychiatry at Allegheny General Hospital in Pittsburgh. Schuster has also been involved in the development of behavioral health services for a regional integrated delivery system.

Schuster received a bachelor's degree from Washington University in St. Louis in 1980 and graduated from the University of Louisville School of Medicine in 1985. He completed training in psychiatry and received an M.B.A. degree from the University of Pittsburgh in 1989. Schuster is board certified in general psychiatry with added qualifications in geriatric psychiatry and addiction psychiatry.

Schuster has published several articles and book chapters and presented papers about managed care and emergency psychiatry at several regional and national meetings. His current academic interests are the components of cost-effective clinical assessments and the effect of managed care on academic departments of psychiatry.

Mark R. Lovell, Ph.D., is the director of the section of psychology and neuropsychology in the Department of Psychiatry at Allegheny General Hospital in Pittsburgh. Lovell completed his doctorate in clinical psychology at the Finch University of Health Sciences at the Chicago Medical School in 1984. He also completed a clinical psychology internship at the University of Nebraska Medical

Center in 1984 and a postdoctoral fellowship in clinical neuropsychology at the University of Nebraska Medical School in 1985.

Lovell is an associate professor of psychiatry at the Pittsburgh campus of Allegheny University of the Health Sciences. There he has been actively involved in the development of both the clinical psychology internship program and the psychiatry residency program. Lovell's academic interests include training in psychology and the neuropsychological assessment of traumatically brain-injured patients. He has published numerous articles, books, and book chapters about clinical psychology and neuropsychology. Lovell recently developed programs for the neuropsychological assessment of athletes after concussion. He serves as a consultant to the National Football League and several colleges and universities.

Anthony M. Trachta, M.S.W., received his degree in social work from the University of Maryland in 1973. He has spent more than twenty years in various endeavors in behavioral healthcare. He is director of managed care at Western Psychiatric Institute and Clinic (WPIC) in Pittsburgh, where he just completed the managed care component of the residency training program. Trachta also recently wrote two book chapters on training issues for social work and ethics in capitation.

Trachta previously served as vice president for clinical services for InterCare in Pittsburgh. There he participated in the development of programs and services in behavioral healthcare as well as managed care in the Pittsburgh market. He has worked as a private practitioner and consultant and has presented papers at several local, state, and national conferences.

Trachta was recently elected to the board of directors of the Association for Ambulatory Behavioral Healthcare. He is involved in the development of a not-for-profit HMO that intends to partner with counties for a regional request for proposal for psychiatric services. He also has been working on formation of a managed care organization (MCO) and an integrated delivery system.

The Contributors

Mark G. Fuller, M.D., F.A.C.P., is the medical director of Green Spring of Western Pennsylvania, a division of Blue Cross of Western Pennsylvania. He is also a clinical associate professor of psychiatry at the Medical College of Pennsylvania and Hahnemann University. He is board certified in psychiatry and internal medicine. Fuller is also qualified in addiction psychiatry from the American Board of Psychiatry and Neurology and has been certified as a specialist in addiction medicine by the American Society of Addiction Medicine. He is the author of several scientific articles, book chapters, and other publications and has lectured extensively at regional and national conferences. He also serves as a reviewer for many scientific journals, including the *Annals of Internal Medicine*, the *American Journal on Addictions*, *General Hospital Psychiatry*, *Psychiatric Services*, the *Journal of Neuropsychiatry and Clinical Neurosciences*, and the *International Journal of Psychiatry in Medicine*.

Marcia Kaplan, M.D., was born and raised in Dallas, Texas, where she completed medical training at the University of Texas Southwestern Medical School and neurology residency at Parkland Hospital. After beginning training in psychiatry in Dallas, she completed her residency at the University of Cincinnati, and has been on the faculty there since graduation in 1988. Kaplan has served as attending psychiatrist on a teaching unit at University Hospital in Cincinnati and as the medical director for University Psychiatric Services and University Managed Care since 1990. She is an advanced candidate at the Cincinnati Psychoanalytic Institute.

David B. Shaw, Ph.D., is the director of the clinical psychology internship and coordinator of outpatient adult psychological services in the Department of Psychiatry of Allegheny General Hospital in Pittsburgh. He is an assistant professor of psychiatry at Allegheny campus of the Medical College of Pennsylvania and

Hahnemann University. Shaw has held positions as assistant director of clinical training, coordinator of outpatient substance abuse treatment services, and coordinator of a schizophrenia research unit for the Department of Veterans Affairs Medical Center in Pittsburgh. He also has been a clinical instructor in psychiatry (psychology) at the University of Pittsburgh School of Medicine. Shaw completed his doctorate in clinical psychology at Texas Tech University and his internship at the Pittsburgh Veterans Administration Consortium. His previous publications address information processing in schizophrenia.

Carole J. Taylor, M.S.N., R.N.C.S., is an independent consultant and psychotherapist and is the former vice president of quality management and patient services for a private behavioral healthcare corporation. Taylor is also on the faculty at the University of Pittsburgh, Waynesburg College, and the Community College of Allegheny County. She is a winner of the Sigma Theta Tau International Society of Nursing's Nursing Leadership Award and a member of several professional organizations including the Pennsylvania Organization of Nurse Executives and Psychiatric Nurse Executives, Inc. Taylor's areas of professional interest include quality management as it pertains to community mental health and Medicaid HMOs, program development, psychotherapy and clinical supervision, and staff development and training. She earned her bachelor's degree in nursing from Slippery Rock University and her master's degree in psychiatric mental health nursing from the University of Pittsburgh.

Deborah A. Teplow, Ph.D., is executive director of the Institute for Behavioral Healthcare (IBH), a nonprofit organization with a mission to improve the quality and structure of behavioral healthcare through innovative, cutting-edge clinical training activities, executive education conferences, educational services, and health research. Teplow is also active in the development of high-tech solutions to the challenges of provider and patient education and training through her work as a member of the projects steering committee of the Bay Area Multimedia Technology Alliance in Silicon Valley, California. Her contributions to provider education have included the production of clinical training modules for major MCOs, collaboration with MCOs on research projects focusing on provider education, and numerous written works on innovations in clinical education instructional design and strategies.

Before joining IBH, Teplow taught at the college level and did educational consulting for the public education system in California. She holds a doctorate in humanities with a subspecialty in education from Stanford University.

Ole J. Thienhaus, M.D., MBA, was born in West Germany and studied chemistry and premedicine at the University of Freiburg. He graduated from medical school in 1978 at the Free University of Berlin after an exchange year at the University of Dublin, Trinity College. He started residency training in surgery in 1978, but changed to psychiatry in 1980 while starting a second-year residency at the University of Cincinnati. He completed a fellowship in geriatric psychiatry, earned an M.B.A. degree, and was appointed to the faculty there in 1985. Thienhaus was appointed vice chairman of the department in 1990 and was directly involved in redesigning the financial structure of his department and the associated practice corporation. His research has focused primarily on dementia and, increasingly, issues of healthcare delivery systems. He has published more than fifty papers and book chapters and one book.

In January 1996, Thienhaus became chairman of the department of psychiatry and behavioral sciences at the University of Nevada. He is a fellow of the American Psychiatric Association (APA), board certified in general and geriatric psychiatry, and certified by the APA in administrative psychiatry.

Index